HORN
of
HONOR

HORNS
of
HONOR

REGAINING THE SPIRIT
OF THE PAGAN HORNED GOD

FREDERICK THOMAS ELWORTHY

EDITED AND INTRODUCED BY

RAVEN GRIMASSI

WEISERBOOKS
San Francisco, CA / Newburyport, MA

This edition first published in 2013 by Weiser Books.
Red Wheel/Weiser, LLC
With offices at:
665 Third Street, Suite 400
San Francisco, CA 94107
www.redwheelweiser.com

ISBN: 978-1-57863-543-6

Library of Congress Cataloging-in-Publication Data available upon request.

Cover design by Jim Warner
Interior by Kathryn Sky-Peck
Typeset in Adobe Garamond

Printed in Canada
FR

10 9 8 7 6 5 4 3 2 1

CONTENTS

INTRODUCTION
BY RAVEN GRIMASSI

ANIMAL HORNS HAVE LONG been an important component of ritual, magic, religious, and spiritual traditions. The average person in contemporary mainstream society is likely to be surprised that horns still play such a role in modern times. Today's Pagans still regard horns as a symbol of power, fertility, and protection. They are worn by many Pagan priests and priestesses, and modern-day shamans. Horns also appear in a large number of Witchcraft rites. The antlers of a stag are among the most popular choices. Antlers, unlike horns, are shed annually, connecting with the old Pagan theme of venerating the cycle of the renewal of life within nature.

Modern Paganism is the envisioned return of humankind to a relationship with nature in which people live in "common cause" with her. Pagans regard the earth as The Great Mother and believe that nature is sentient (as opposed to the scientific view that the earth is simply a perpetual motion machine with no consciousness). It is a popular Pagan belief that divinity expresses itself as a variety of goddesses and gods.

In modern Wicca there is an emphasis on a mated pair of deities—the Goddess and the God. A great deal of literature exists pertaining to the Goddess, but by comparison there is very little about the God. This is most obvious when it comes to books about the

"Stag-Horned God" who appears in many Wiccan systems and in some Witchcraft traditions. Why is there so little available about the venerable God and his noble horns?

In the late spring of 2012, my publisher offered me the opportunity to work on the re-publication of a book titled *Horns of Honor*, by Frederick Thomas Elworthy. I had read this nineteenth-century book quite some time ago and have long appreciated the many gems of pre-Christian elements residing within it. My publisher and I shared the vision of producing something for the contemporary Pagan community that has deep and strong roots in the foundational ideas that contribute to modern beliefs and practices. Therefore, we set out to make this book widely available. But in doing so, we needed to ensure its relevancy for a new readership.

In essence, this book is about the meaning, importance, and symbolism of animal horns in Pagan antiquity (as well as the regard for horns later on in the era of Christianity) as presented to us through the eyes of a nineteenth-century archaeologist. By way of the pages of his book, we are introduced to the foundational beliefs in horns as representations of personal status within a community, including rulership and nobility. In contrast to this theme, the author also presents horn symbolism as tokens and gestures of dishonor and disgrace. The latter theme appears centuries into the Christian era and was cleverly applied to a campaign of misinformation intended to discourage people from embracing Pagan beliefs and practices. It worked exceedingly well.

My primary mission in this re-publication of *Horns of Honor* is to provide a new introduction along with commentaries that clarify and, in some cases, update various views held by the original author.

Although modern scholars are sure to object to some of Elworthy's arguments, there is a great deal of valuable material and insights that are worthy of reflective thought. What Elworthy has passed on to the contemporary Pagan community through his book is the redemption of the horn as a positive symbol. In order to appreciate the message of his book, as opposed to becoming distracted and burdened by its minor flaws, we must take into account the writer himself.

Frederick Thomas Elworthy (1830–1907) was a product of the nineteenth century, its views, politics, and notions. This can be problematic to modern ways of thinking, and therefore, measures have been taken to minimize such an effect in this edition. It should be noted that modern academics give little credence to the views of nineteenth-century writers. Since today's academic methodology is more rigid and demanding than was that of this previous period, there is a tendency to dismiss the conclusions of nineteenth-century writers despite any individual's education and experience.

Elworthy was a philologist and antiquarian book collector. Philology is the study of literary texts and written records in order to establish their original form and authenticity (as well as the determination of word meanings). Elworthy was born in Wellington, Somerset, and later in life he became interested in the dialects and antiquities of western Somerset and eastern Devon. In 1886, he published *The West Somerset Word-Book*, a 900-page glossary of dialect words. He also studied folk magic and popular superstition during his extensive stays in such places as Spain and Italy.

In 1887, Elworthy joined the British Association for the Advancement of Science, and by 1893, he was a member of its General

Committee. He was also a member of the council of the Philological Society and the editor for the Somersetshire Archaeological and Natural History Society. He was elected Fellow of the Society of Antiquaries in 1900.

Elworthy was a skilled linguist and also demonstrated proficiency as a draughtsman, engraver, and watercolorist. He was a prominent churchman well known for his personal and financial support in the building of All Saints' Church at Wellington. He served as a churchwarden, an active member of the Wellington school board, and a local magistrate. Elworthy was also a member of the Council of the Folk-lore Society and was well known for his lectures on the significance of surviving elements of old animistic corn-cults in the United Kingdom, Greece, and Egypt. In addition, he was a prominent Freemason of the region of Somerset.

As previously mentioned, Elworthy was very much involved with the Church. His strong Christian views appear in various statements he makes within this text. You will find the term "Our Lord" repeated in several chapters, by which Elworthy means Jesus Christ, and obviously not the Horned God of Pagan belief. It is also made clear in the text that Elworthy regards Christianity as the means by which "Pagan error" was corrected. However, at the same time he is not hostile toward Pagan beliefs, and the bulk of this book is remarkably fair in its view on old Pagan spiritual and religious themes.

An interesting biblical theme involves the analogy of sheep, representing followers of Jesus, the Good Shepherd, and goats symbolizing non-followers, the Pagans. Sheep will follow anyone who seems to be leading, but goats are difficult to control. Their independent nature became a theme for disobedience and resistance to Christianity. The Church saw this situation as a result of demonic influence directed and overseen by the Devil. Elworthy spends an entire chapter on the connection between the horns of the Devil and goat horns. As we know, the Devil was historically believed to be worshipped by witches, and Pagans were thought to be deceived by demons into believing in false gods.

Paganism never had a true connection to the Devil, and its people worshipped many gods and goddesses together. In modern Paganism the major emphasis is upon a goddess as opposed to a god. When something beneficial takes place in a person's life, the expression of gratitude is most commonly directed to the Goddess ("Thank the Goddess!") as opposed to the God (either by himself or as consort to the Goddess). However, in many forms of modern Pagan practice, the God is well represented as a key and central figure. I believe that this current edition of *Horns of Honor* will help strengthen appreciation of the Horned God in contemporary Paganism.

One of the favored aspects of the God in modern times is the Stag-Horned God (sometimes called the Antlered One or the Stag Antler God). He is most commonly associated with northern European cultures of the past, although gods with antlers were also known in southern Europe. The Stag-Horned God is often depicted as the consort of the Moon Goddess. However, modern Paganism involves many deities and not one single mated pair.

Among the gods of contemporary Paganism, there is the ancient Celtic deity known as Cernunnus. In ancient art he appears with stag antlers and is associated with fertility. He is also connected with the Underworld, and in this aspect he is a guide or escort of the dead on their journey. The being known as Herne is also frequently shown with antlers. He is connected to the legendary Wild Hunt, and as such he represents the primal forces at work outside the cultivated and "civilized" regions maintained by humankind. I will have more to say about him later.

Other types of animal horns feature in the history of Pagan beliefs and practices. Among them are two in particular, the bull and the goat. Elworthy devotes most of his chapters to these specific horns and their associated deities with a focus upon Dionysus and Pan, but gods from various other cultures are included as well.

In contemporary Paganism, when we consider horns, the emphasis appears to be upon the antlers of a stag. Although worn as a headdress predominantly by men, some women also choose to don the antlers or some other type of animal horn. Men frequently wear horns as a symbol of strength and power, typically in connection with a horned god they venerate. They can also be a symbol of status or present the wearer as a shaman. While some women use horned headdresses for similar reasons, many wear them to invoke a sense of liberation, free-spiritedness, playfulness, and even raw sensuality. Others wear horns to align with a specific god or goddess.

Aligning or connecting with the nature of one's deity is a very ancient theme. Ingesting of the essence of a deity is among the oldest concepts in spiritual practices. In the case of Dionysus, wine is consumed in order to invoke the spirit of the god. This principle later shows up in Christianity through the idea of claiming rebirth through the mythos of the death and resurrection of Jesus observed in the formal rite of communion in which the "body and blood" of Christ are symbolically consumed. When we consider that horns were once drinking vessels, the idea of "communion" takes on an interesting perspective.

There are older rooted ideas we need to explore—whether appearing in pre-Christian or Christian culture—in order to better understand the symbolism of the horn. Elworthy doesn't include the antlers of the stag in his book, but I feel the portrait is incomplete without them. Stags appear in very old myths and legends, particularly in northern Europe. Among them the White Stag is of particular mystical meaning and symbolism associated with the Otherworld and the Faery Realm of pre-Christian lore. Its appearance is often a sign that entry to or from such realms is at hand. The stag itself featured prominently in ancient cultures and is currently linked to modern traditions of Paganism and Witchcraft. One example is that formerly taught by Robert Cochrane, which focuses on the roebuck, a specific type of deer.

In Cochrane's system or those branching from it, the stag is a symbol of leadership and sacrifice. The idea of leadership is a theme that Elworthy links to royal crowns, which he believes are ultimately fashioned after horn headdresses with the spikes in the crown being stylized horn tips. The idea comes into focus when we think about the custom of mounting a stag's head on a wall, complete with a full rack of antlers. Its display suggests the skills of the hunter separated out from others, a "king of the hunters" statement for all to behold.

In some systems of Pagan Witchcraft, the stag represents the "Grand Master" or "Horned One" of the Forest. This later evolved into the Goat-Horned God of the Sabbat, a classic design popularized by the occultist Eliphas Lévi. Images from the Middle Ages and the Renaissance depicted the Lord of the Sabbat with bull horns and labeled him the Devil. Elworthy correctly points out that no physical description of the Devil exists in the Bible, and yet early Christian images portray him with features identical to those of various Pagan gods.

The Church incorporated Pagan imagery into its concepts of evil and those beings it called demons. However, certain previously sacred concepts were handled in a gentler manner so that Pagan ways could be absorbed and adapted into Christianity and its converts could settle into familiar surroundings. One such concept was that of the White Stag. Saints such as Eustace, Hubert, Julian, and Felix are connected to variations on the White Stag story. In general the tale goes that the saint is hunting (usually prior to becoming a saint or even a Christian) and encounters a white stag. The stag comes forward bearing a crucifix set in its antlers. A human voice then speaks from the object and addresses the hunter, identifying itself as the Christ. The person is overcome by this and has a conversion experience. The saint is then associated with the White Stag, a profound pre-connection within the culture that transfers veneration over to the saint. However, the root concept of the sacred stag remains Pagan in nature.

In the case of St. Eustace, after he accepts the White Stag as Christ, he is told that great tribulations await him because of his conversion. He is further informed that many temptations will come to test his devotion. St. Eustace accepts all of this and asks only to be given the patience to suffer through to the end. The White Stag replies that he need only be strong and courageous, and he will not be forsaken. Here we see the classic mythos of the sacrificial figure associated with a horned beast.

Another figure who borrows and adapts Pagan themes within the Christian era is Herne the Hunter. He wears antlers and is accompanied by a train of souls; the latter is an older concept associated with a goddess. One of her names in the famous Canon Episcopi is Diana, a goddess of the hunt and of the moon. One of her cult animals was the stag. She is said to ride at night with a horde of followers, a classic folkloric tale related to the ghost train of the spirits of the dead.

There are several versions of the tale of Herne the Hunter. Most of them are similar, but the primary exceptions are Herne's two deaths and why he died the second one. The basic tale begins with Herne as a skilled hunter accompanying King Richard II on a stag hunt. At one point a stag startles the king's horse, and he is thrown to the ground. The stag charges the king, but Herne places himself between the two. The stag fatally gores Herne, who kills his slayer before he dies.

Suddenly, a dark figure appears on the scene and introduces himself as Philip Urswick. In some tales he is a doctor, and in others he is a wizard or the Devil. Urswick offers to return Herne to life, and the king accepts. Urswick has the stag's antlers removed and placed on Herne's head. Herne is then carried off to Urswick's dwelling place in the forest. A month later the resurrected Herne comes back to King Richard, who rejoices at his return and appoints him Chief Hunter in the Realm.

Unfortunately, Herne's fellow hunters become jealous of him and devise a plot to turn the king against Herne, and also pits Urswick against him as well. The lies and deception cause Herne to fall into disfavor and to lose his honor. In one tale he is so distraught that he hangs himself from an oak tree in the forest. Here again we see the theme of sacrifice woven into the tale.

Near the end of the story, Urswick learns of the betrayal of the hunters. He lures them into the forest where Herne appears to them. Urswick then forces them to swear an oath of loyalty to Herne. Later on, the king learns of the hunters' misdeeds. Herne demands vengeance, and the king orders them slain. As the story closes, the souls of the hunters are doomed to ride with Herne on the Wild Hunt through the forests around Windsor Castle.

In some modern circles, Herne is regarded as the old Horned God of the Forest, who is transformed into a folkloric spirit that haunts the Windsor region. The idea of a stag-horned god became central in early Wiccan systems that claimed a time-honored connection. Supporters pointed to such figures as the Paleolithic image of the "Stag man" painted on a cave wall at Trois Frères, Ariège. Anthropologist Margaret Murray even argued that Witchcraft is the surviving remnant of an ancient religion that venerated the goddess Diana and her horned consort. However, modern scholars completely reject her work in this field.

Murray wrote the introduction to a book titled *Witchcraft Today,* by Gerald Gardner. Credited with launching what many people refer to as the Wiccan movement, Gardner put forth the idea that in past times a Witchcraft priest wore stag antlers or bull horns, a mask, and even animal skins in order to impersonate the Old God of the Forest. While most modern scholars dismiss Gardner's claims of a tradition surviving from antiquity, the basic concepts in Gardnerian Witchcraft are not purely modern ideas.

Gardner's idea of a man wearing horns as a sign of his priesthood connects well with Elworthy's views on the headdress translated into a crown. It is Gardner's mention of the bull horns sometimes worn by the priest that allows us to directly connect with the type of horns examined by Elworthy. My own research has revealed no less a divinity connected with bull horns than the god Dionysus. Therefore, we will start here to root out the ancient importance of the horn that, according to Elworthy, later became the crown.

Like most Pagan deities, Dionysus is greatly misrepresented in the public arena. Many people associate him with drunkenness and debauchery, and his ancient followers, the maenads, with violent and crazed behavior. While it appears true that the ancient cult eventually deteriorated over time, the original model focused on ecstasy through divine possession. The goal of the Dionysian rites was divine intoxication as opposed to simple alcohol or drug intoxication. However, such substances were part of the rites to serve as catalysts to the process of receiving divine ecstasy.

The Church has long held to the vision of Pagan rites and the Witches' Sabbat as gatherings in which "moral abandonment" is performed in the presence of a horned entity such as Satan. Elworthy spends a chapter on the subject of the Devil's horns without presenting a cohesive explanation. When we examine early images of the Devil, and demons, it is easy to recognize various aspects, such as the beaked nose, which earlier appeared on Charun, the feared god of death. The body shape is either goat-like or donkey-like, styled after Pan and Dionysus. Often we see small wings on the feet that are earlier found on the god Hermes in his aspect as consort of the dead. Bat wings, or dragon wings, often complete the imagery and are added to associate demons and the Devil with dreaded creatures and the night. It is noteworthy that Dionysus Zagreus was said to have been born with dragon wings. Such deliberate associations served to wrongfully debase the Pagan symbolism of the horn as a noble sign of power and leadership.

Elworthy notes that by the sixteenth century regard for the horn was almost completely transformed into something negative. The wearing of horns, once looked upon with pride, honor, and victory, became reduced to symbolizing ignorance and disgrace. In this light, Elworthy tries to connect the Italian word *scornare* (literally meaning to be deprived of horns) with the English word *scorn*, which denotes shame or contempt.

As noted earlier, at the core of Elworthy's book is his theory that the crown evolved from primitive horned headdresses. However, many of the earliest crowns of record are actually circlets of various plant types. Some examples are laurel leaves, olive leaves, and ivy. Ivy is of particular interest for our purposes because it brings us back to Dionysus and connects back to kingship, divine rule, and the wearing of horns.

Many classic images of Dionysus present him wearing a crown of grape leaves, grapes, and even ivy. Among his earliest forms, Dionysus was known as the "God of the Trees"—the woodland realm of the goat. One of his divine aspects is Dionysus Dendrites, the classic image of whom shows the god cradling a tree in his arms. Dionysus has been called the Sovereign of Nature and the reconciler of our celestial and terrestrial natures. Social anthropologist James Frazer wrote in his book *The Golden Bough* about connections between kings, the spirit of the land, and king-figures from various cultures. A popular aspect of the Arthurian mythos regards the well-being of the land as intimately connected with the well-being of the king.

During the period in which Elworthy wrote his book, Dionysus was often viewed in his diminished form of Bacchus, the Roman aspect of Dionysus. Therefore, the complex nature of Dionysus evaded Elworthy when he addressed the topic of the Devil's horns. Had Elworthy also known that Dionysus was a god who died, was resurrected, and ascended long before the story of the Christ, he might have had more to say in terms of the Christian vilification of the horned gods of Paganism. The Church's need to transplant horns onto their Devil and to present horns in such a negative context became a powerful force through which to control the religious lives of people out of fear.

In the book *Thinking with Demons: The Idea of Witchcraft in Early Modern Europe,* author Stuart Clark makes reference to the Witches' Sabbat and its connection to the Bacchanalia (rites associated with Dionysus/Bacchus). In the sixteenth century, Pierre Crespet, prior of the French Celestines, claimed that the Bacchanalia and the Sabbat were in fact one rite. About a century later, this idea was elaborated upon by two Frenchmen, Francois de Rosset and Francois Hedelin, abbé d'Aubignac. Each claimed that both festivals were presided over by Bacchus, who they state is a devil appearing in the form of a goat. They further claimed that the celebrants of these rites were devils and witches. Rosset stated that the ceremonies continued down through the ages though demonic transmission and were nothing else but what is now called the Witches' Sabbat.

As mentioned earlier, occultist Eliphas Lévi popularized the "Sabbatic Goat" sometimes identified with Baphomet. Elworthy points to goat horns and the grafting of them onto the imagery of the Devil. He also mentions the Knights Templar who were accused of worshipping the Devil under the name Baphomet. The most popular image of Baphomet depicts him as a large goat with bat or dragon wings. He is always seated and shown with an erection in the shape of a caduceus. Between his goat horns is a lighted torch, and his arms are extended in opposite directions, with one hand pointing up and the other down, meant to symbolize his ability to draw upon and direct both celestial and terrestrial forces.

Elworthy seems less concerned about the various symbolic elements associated with the Devil and spends most of his focus on the mere appearance of the Satan. He does not appear to be interested in what contributed to the depiction or nature of the Devil outside of sporting horns. Elworthy primarily looks to the god Pan as the model for the Devil, and in this way elements of sexuality are introduced, setting the basis for allegations of orgies at the Sabbat. In another chapter, the author mentions a hand gesture known in Italy as "*mano cornuto*" (the horned hand) that is sometimes displayed behind a man's back to indicate that his wife is intimately involved with another man. Here we see transference of the horn and its associate with sexual freedom—but always in a negative manner.

Elworthy spends the last portion of his book examining the connection between hand gestures and animal horns. He includes drawings of ancient sculptures and images of hands decorated with a variety of symbols. Some of them represent "signs of blessings" of while others have more mystical or magical symbolism. It is interesting to note that the posture of these hands from Pagan times are identical with the position of hands later appearing in Christian art showing Jesus or a saint giving a blessing. Baphomet is shown with one that is frequently seen in Christian iconography. It should be remembered that such hand signs predate Christianity.

The hand was already used in the art of cave paintings and is prominent in magical systems of the Middle Ages and Renaissance. In some forms of Witchcraft, the hand is placed upon a hearth to swear an oath and to evoke spirits of the dead. In the case of the latter, spirits who died violent deaths in five different ways are called forth as each finger of the hand is raised. Is this another display of the animal horn as a sign of power, or is it some mystical evocation in which the five fingers of the hand represent a crown or magical authority?

Several hand sculptures are presented as the "hand of Sabazius" who was a Greek god identified with Dionysus. It is Elworthy's belief that such hands were placed next to or near statues of a goddess or god on a temple setting. In such cases the symbolism of the hand preserves and displays important concepts and themes that belong to the cult of the deity. The designs are understood by members of the sect, and this enhances the religious experience within the temple. Today there is much debate over the meaning of the symbolism that comes down to us from ancient times.

Throughout the various chapters provided by Elworthy in this book, there is a richness of old lore and antiquated views that remained in place well into the early twentieth century. The text can, in part, be regarded as a snapshot of the intellectual period before the science of anthropology became solidified in the next century. In the nineteenth century, anthropology was a young and growing science. Today, twenty-first-century anthropology stands in avowed opposition to the premises of the former period and its school of thinking.

Most modern anthropologists ridicule and reject the views of nineteenth-century anthropologists and folklorists, relegating their findings to the scrap heap of "outdated" and forsaken "mid-Victorian" perspectives. Unfortunately, this approach tends to "throw the baby out with the bath water," and in so doing we are denied something essential—the kernel of truth.

What can we say is true of the ancient Pagan and his or her regard for horns? The longevity of old festivals and celebrations featuring horns is certainly a testament to their cultural importance. One example is the annual Abbots Bromley Horn Dance held in Staffordshire featuring a dance in which people wear antlers and move through the town. Included in the celebration is a musician, a boy carrying a triangle, another with a crossbow, a Fool character, a Hobby Horse, and a man dressed as a Maiden. Another example is the October celebration of the Horn Fair, formerly held at Charlton in Kent, but abolished in 1872. Celebrants wore or carried horns, animal stalls were decorated with horns, and the saying "All's fair at Horn Fair" came about due to the setting aside of inhibitions during the event.

The argument can be raised that such celebrations are simply remnants of hunting rites performed in the belief that they ensured a successful outing. However, we know that various Pagan gods wore horns and antlers, which strongly suggests a religious component. There is little doubt that when the One God came to displace the Many, an intentional severance took place between the practical and religious aspects of horn celebrations.

During the medieval period, many laws, admonishments, and edicts were directed against Pagan practices such as wearing horns, dressing like an animal, and celebrating in Pagan fashion. The persistence of such practices cannot reasonably be due to their festive nature, and must almost certainly point to something much more important. Punishment for these "crimes" was harsh; to risk being caught calls for a greater devotion than mere adherence to custom. Therefore, are we looking at the cause being true devotion to the "Old Gods" of Paganism?

Most modern Pagans care very little about how well modern Paganism matches its ancient counterpart, or even if it does. In other words, modern practitioners feel and experience their ways. They do not rely upon academic validation of their beliefs and practices. Pagans today desire a spiritual path or religion that is less defined and not saddled with specific tenets, doctrine, and dogma.

Critics of modern Pagans accuse them of romanticizing ancient Paganism and misrepresenting it in the contemporary world. It is true that ancient Paganism and its practitioners were different in key ways compared to the mainstream ways of today's Paganism. Life was much harder in ancient times, and survival less assured. Dealing with things such as natural disasters, disease, crop failure, and sick herd animals called for actions that would horrify most modern people. This included live sacrifice in a belief that the gods, spirits, or forces of nature would be appeased. In ancient culture this was not an immoral act. Additionally, ancient Pagans readily defended themselves with violence and were not a people who believed in the "harm none" philosophy that currently exists in some circles.

Although the average modern Pagan is not concerned with historic Paganism in any practical way, unfortunately the view of mainstream society is still problematic for Pagans. It is a word that evokes misunderstanding, fear, and the inescapable knee-jerk reactions from fundamental Christians rooted in prejudgment as opposed to actual personal experience with modern Pagans and their ways. I recall, on more than one occasion, hearing from park officials after they permitted a Pagan gathering that they were amazed to find the park left cleaner than it was when the Pagans arrived for the weekend. Several commented they always feel relieved when they see a Pagan gathering on the schedule as opposed to other organizations that reserve the park. This is personal experience versus prejudgment.

In this light, Elworthy's *Horns of Honor* is of value to the modern Pagan. His writings provide information that counters the misinformation, misjudgment, and ignorance that is all too common in mainstream society. This information can be used to help dismantle the walls of obstruction that stand against the Pagan movement today. By reclaiming and regaining the noble elements of our ancestral beliefs and practices, we can receive sustaining nourishment from our roots. We can move forward with the light that dispels ignorance, which will allow us to reach the place we seek in the world today.

On a final note, I urge the skeptical reader not to accuse Elworthy of fostering pseudo-history. He writes from a period in time when no "official" academic organization postured itself as the safeguard of ultimate truth. Therefore, Elworthy is not trying to rewrite history. Instead, he is examining fragments left in the sands of time, and then he looks from within his own period to make sense of what came to be. It is as noble an approach as is the Pagan spirit of the horn itself.

—RAVEN GRIMASSI
MASSACHUSETTS, 2013

AUTHOR'S INTRODUCTION

THE VERY KIND RECEPTION accorded to my book on *The Evil Eye* has emboldened me, and must be taken as my excuse for appearing again, probably for the last time, before the public.

Although I have now scarcely touched upon the former subject, yet its presence is so manifest in every phase of ancient and uncultured life of to-day, that just as all roads lead to Rome, so every study of manners or beliefs seems inevitably to lead up to, or at least to be closely influenced by, that all-prevailing fear.

As before, I have no theories to propound or to support, and wherever in these pages anything of the nature of a thesis may appear, I have only to say that it is simply put forward as the result of a conclusion from purely inductive processes.

I presume to be no more than an observer and noter of such facts as from time to time come in my way; consequently, as before, inconsistencies will be found, but with these I am not concerned; nature, as viewed by us, is most inconsistent, and my business is with facts, whether they tell for or against the conclusions at which personally I have arrived.

In whatever direction of study one may set out, it is utterly impossible to pursue a definitely circumscribed line—the historian must branch into geography, the geologist into zoology, and hence arise many paradoxes. Without comprehending a word of it, I have lately been asked if I knew anything of "Geometrical Chemistry," and without a blush confessed my ignorance; so in my first chapter I have to bring the reader face to face with "Pictorial Etymology," and yet I hope that the curious facts, to be verified by anybody, will be so evident as to dissolve that paradox. So too I hope it may become as evident to the reader as it has to the writer, that the crown of royalty has for one of its elements the horns of Egyptian deities.

One object I have kept steadily in view, especially in the final chapters—that of placing the evidence, whether for or against, in juxtaposition, and particularly when the facts dealt with depend upon pictorial illustration; and I venture to hope that by so marshalling the objects side by side, not only will the interest of the reader be better served, but he will thereby have the opportunity of judging the conclusions I have come to from the like comparison.

An apology is needed for the quality of some of the sketches. They were made at different times, often at long intervals, and frequently under very adverse circumstances. Moreover, I do not pretend to any skill, and only use my own productions when no better are obtainable.

The subject of the *Dischi Sacri*, the antitypes of the *Mano Pantea*, is of considerable interest and importance to the classical mythologist, for the reason that the objects themselves, though very common and clearly belonging to the everyday life of the ages to which they belonged, are unnoticed in any contemporary literature, while the great number of the *Dischi Sacri*, as well as of the symbolic hands, seems to open a new field for the study of archaeologists. If, then, the true function of archaeology be that of enabling us to realise more truly the life of the past, I submit with all diffidence that this little book will not have failed if it suggests to other and abler students a fresh branch of interesting research.

I have only further to express my obligation and cordial thanks to Mr. G. E. Marindin for several corrections in Latinity, which after fifty years of neglect had naturally become well-nigh a reminiscence. For several valuable suggestions in mythology I am further deeply indebted to him.

While writing these lines, a curious comment upon my remarks upon the persistent charges of ritual murder against early Christians and Templars appears in the trial at Nameszto in Hungary, noticed in this week's *Spectator*, where the Jews are alleged to have murdered a boy to obtain his blood for ritual purposes.

—Fred. T. Elworthy
Foxdown, January 1, 1900

CHAPTER I.

INTRODUCTORY

I N THE FOLLOWING PAGES it is assumed that all attempts at decoration, whether of the person in the way of dress, or of pattern, shown by curved lines or other evidence of design, however crude, upon inanimate objects, had in their origin some definite idea or fact which it was intended to illustrate. In other words, no pictorial device of primitive man beyond the simplest straight strokes upon his pottery was simply arbitrary; but however rude in execution, every stroke or figure had a meaning of its own. In fact we believe that generally all attempts at decoration were more or less ideographic, and in support of this belief, it is only necessary here to refer to the familiar example in the writing of Egypt—the wavy line denoting water—and to point out that it is practically the same line so often seen upon a variety of archaic vessels for holding liquid.

Thus when untutored man wished to indicate the sun he drew a circle, and often improved on it by adding radiating strokes like a wheel. When he wanted to indicate the moon he drew or scratched something like a crescent.

In these days, however, when the original idea has been long forgotten, and the decorative item has developed into a very remote likeness to its prototype, it is extremely difficult to trace back the elaborate productions of modern civilisation to their progenitors in the rude devices of our remote forefathers.

The books on Art and its origin are legion, and no attempt will here be made even to touch the fringe of those great subjects. Instead of doing so, and in support of the assumption above made, the reader is referred to *The Evolution of Decorative Art*, by Henry Balfour, 1893, and to *Evolution in Art*, by A. C. Haddon (Contemporary Science Series, 1895). On this subject we specially recommend a valuable article in *Good Words* for September, 1896, by A. E. Farman and G. Clarke Nuttall, entitled "The Lost Soul of Patterns." Many familiar devices are illustrated and accounted for in a most ingenious manner. All these modern writers deal exhaustively and convincingly with this branch of the question, with abundant illustration. We shall hope to show, however, that difficult as is the task of general identification of modern designs with their prototypes among primaeval ones, yet in the vast majority of cases which can certainly be proved to be the survivals of ancient forms, the original picture or object had a very distinctive use, and was worn, or depicted, or sculptured, so as continually to act as a preventive of the ever-dreaded evil against which all magic was primarily directed.

Reasoning then from the known to the unknown, it may, without presumption, be maintained that in their incidence all ornament and all decoration had their ultimate purpose in the supposed prophylactic power of the subject delineated, or perhaps of the object on which the decoration was placed. The ornamentation itself in the first place was intended to help in attracting the eye, and so to divert the first glance from the wearer of the decoration—for the danger was past after that.

All ornament and all disfigurement naturally appeal to the eye alone, and so far as personal decoration is concerned experience convinces us that in every age, whether ancient or modern, the head has among mankind ever been the object of both honour and dishonour; the part on which his taste for ornament has been first displayed. The crown, the distinctive sign of glory, of honour, and of kingly power, or the wreath of victory, just as much as the ashes of mourning and the fool's cap, are placed upon the head, the recognised seat of both intelligence and folly. Besides its manifold use in a literal sense, the head is constantly taken to represent the entire individual. Not only was succour of an enemy declared to be heaping coals of fire on his head, but in many other ways the head is used figuratively in Scripture; while in modern literature its use has grown and developed to a degree quite extraordinary to those who have not examined the recent marshalling of evidence.[1]

Nature has adorned the head of the most familiar of our domestic birds with the *crista*, that distinguishing excrescence which surely first impressed its form upon the head-gear of ancient Greek heroes;[2] while in later times it gave its name to the figure or device worn upon the helmet of a knight in the days of chivalry, and has thence come down to us as a well-known term in heraldry. The various objects we now call crests were, in the Middle Ages, very differently regarded by those who wore them as compared with what they are to-day. Then they were worn as ensigns of high distinction and honour, and especially of personal prowess, so that their use was restricted to a comparatively few persons of eminence and of martial renown; but in these later times "crests" have become just as common and just as valueless as the paper on which they are stamped; while they are of as little real significance as the modern term "esquire"; until at last they have often sunk to be the mere fanciful and fantastic ornaments of the vulgar, the ignorant, and the *nouveau riche*.

The origin of crests, however, takes us far behind their name, far behind even the beginnings of the Latin tongue which gave rise to it. The crest usually depicted upon the head of Greek heroes, we see at a glance, is but a conventionalised imitation of the *Crista Galli*, showing that the idea in their day was precisely the same as that which survived until the Middle Ages, an idea which grew and became so modified, or developed by widespread use and fancy, that at last any

distinctive ornament on a knight's head took the name of that appendage, and became his crest.

The head-dress here depicted (Fig. 1) is only one of several similar upon a sarcophagus in the British Museum, recently brought from Clazomenæ, in Asia Minor, and represents a Greek warrior of the seventh century BC. The

Fig. 1.

crest is here so exaggerated as to be even more important and conspicuous than the helmet itself, but we see in it the same type which we recognise as the well-known, conventional one for heroes upon Greek vases.[3] Other special points in this illustration will be referred to later on.

We have here also a rough sketch (Fig. 2) of a Roman cavalry soldier from the engravings of Montfaucon, showing the conventional as well as the composite character of the crest. In the much later classic times to which this crest belongs, we note that

Fig. 2.

it is mounted high over all, even above a protective amulet in the shape of a bird, but we cannot fail to see in it the general form of the same conventional cock's comb which, often so much exaggerated by the Greeks, still continues to ornament the helmet of the modern dragoon, no less than that of the civilian fireman, and is even found somewhat belittled on the less civil policeman. This crest still perpetuates, in the shape of a concrete ornament, the old idea of victory, so graphically expressed in the slang of to-day, "Cock county," "Cock of the walk," "Cock of the school"; and more figuratively also in the literary cockscomb. We see it, too, in him who by his rank or profession wears a cockade, or a cocked hat, or in one who struts and assumes the victorious air of the ideal cockscomb. We all know the attitude of many a bird during his song, particularly the lark, which has been so well described as the "raising of the ornamental plumes during courtship." The fact that natural instinct prompts birds to erect their crest as a sign of conquest, or at least of challenge, seems to point curiously to the same instinct in mankind, whether savage or cultured—he mounts a plume of feathers or a bunch of hair on his head in token of triumph. For example, in New Guinea a tuft of white feathers is mounted upon the head of the warrior who has killed a man. (While in the press Mr. Seligman has kindly furnished the following interesting details as to Papuan head-gear:—

"Distinctions worn for killing a person:

Sepe—White shell forehead-band.

Karai—White cockatoo plumes worn in the hair.

Bina—Upper mandible of *Toucan* worn on the head. This is only worn by a man who has taken life in single combat. (*Toucan* should be hornbill.—C.G.S.)

Tiabe—Plumes of *Paradisea Raggiona* worn on the head.

Representations of the head of a murdered man or woman, or of their private parts, are often carved on clubs by the murderer.")

The reader is asked here to note the bird's beak to imitate a horn on the head of the victor at Bina.

Compare with the above the cockades, plumes, and other ornaments worn on their heads by all soldiers in full "war paint," whether officers or privates.

Long before the Romans, or even the Greeks, of history, we have shown, elsewhere, a more or less elaborate head adornment to have been the distinguishing mark of the Egyptian gods and goddesses. Just as the kind of crest worn by an armoured knight in days of chivalry was usually intended to denote some trait in his character, some ideal he was pursuing, or to symbolise some event in his career; so in the earlier days of Egyptian history the devices placed upon the heads of deities were the symbols of what were believed to be their distinctive attributes; and we submit with all confidence that it was certainly the survival of the same notion that crested the gods, which caused, in crusading days, the device to be mounted upon a knight's helmet. The notion had of course come down to chivalry, through a long succession of ages, and of peoples, all mounting "crests" upon their fighting men.

Certain ornamental devices worn upon the head, became in course of time identified with certain great offices, civil as well as military, and, without waiting to dwell upon the several steps of the development, it is easy to see how various caps of office or dignity, such, for instance, as the mitre, and, still more, that very composite head-dress we now call a crown, came to be the distinguishing mark of the chief priest, of the victor, and so of the king (the man who can, and the man who kens). In later times, when feudal lords arose, who were really little kings, there was devised for them an inferior badge, a head-dress of similar type and intent, but denoting their lesser rule—the coronet.

The greatest of the gods in every mythology have been personifications of the most conspicuous heavenly bodies—the sun and moon.[4] These were the visible sources of life and heat, and, even in the face of Sir Norman Lockyer, we venture to maintain that to them, and not to Sirius, was the highest worship accorded by all nations. One and all looked upon them as living; and, in their chief attributes, they were both regarded mainly as beneficent beings. For our immediate purpose it will be most convenient to confine ourselves to the gods of Egypt and to those of later ages which we can identify with them, for, without going further back, we must start with the premise that so much of the religious systems now existing in Europe as cannot be clearly shown to be primaeval, indigenous (if we may use the word) in the genus *homo*, has, in a very large measure, descended to us from Egypt, thence passing through the various modifications of Greek and Roman paganism, yet at the same time deeply influenced by much Oriental belief and practice, brought to bear upon and through the Jews.

From this point of view, with all reverence, we look upon Christianity as a great reform, in fact a mighty revolution. [Here Elworthy, as a Christian, holds this prideful but erroneous position.] What was true or valuable in the ancient systems was retained, adapted, and purified; while the grosser part was cast aside [meaning that the arrogation of Pagan beliefs and practices included the rejection of primal connections, nature-based deities, and fertility oriented rites while selecting other aspects the better suited the Church's agenda]. The sun was considered by the ancients as the father, the giver and protector of life. And we cannot fail to see that this notion of generation and protection is well symbolised by the psalmist when he declares "The Lord God is a sun and shield." (Psalm lxxxiv. 11.)

In all ages and by all people we find the sun, however rudely pictured, to be the symbol of the highest divinity; later on we shall show how, in the special device known as the wheel-cross, it has been preserved through long ages of paganism down to the Christianity of to-day, as a sign to denote the might and Godhead of each person of the Blessed Trinity. The moon having been looked upon, at least by the Aryan stock, as the mother of the gods and men, was naturally regarded as the great and beneficent protector of her progeny; consequently, as we should expect, so do we find, that the symbol of her personification is distinguished by the most remarkable of her visible forms, the crescent. [However, it should be noted that in some European cultures, the sun was regarded as a goddess.] This well-known symbol, being placed as a cognisance or crest upon her head, has in all ages denoted the universal, the Celestial Mother, or perhaps rather the type of motherhood, whether known of old as Ishtar, Isis, Artemis, Diana, or, as at present, Madonna.

The crescent upon it, when viewed from the front, gives to the head an appearance of having the horns of a short-horned cow, and from its being so placed upon all moon gods and goddesses, the crescent has got the name of the horned moon. Upon this point enough has been said elsewhere in connection with Hera-Iö, who gave her name to the Bosporus—the passage of the cow. Later on we see that this notion had taken such hold that, instead of the points of a crescent being placed upon the head, we find a natural, realistic treatment: the horns of animals, mostly cows, were placed upon the head, and at last bovine horns themselves, in the concrete (not merely the crescent), became the badge or crest of the moon goddess. Thence it has survived in these Christian days as the symbol of the most compassionate and loving, as well as the most powerful of female beings, of her who in these latter days bears the old-world title Mater Dei.[5] We shall also show that this badge was by no means confined to goddesses in pagan times, but that it distinguished gods as well, and thus explains the expression "Moon gods and goddesses" used above.

Hence, bearing in mind that this godlike crest, at first the emblem only of a powerful deity, came to be looked upon as something in itself that would be effectual; and thus the crescent was considered to be, and was used by men as a protective amulet, thereby becoming a constant appeal for safety to the gods it represented, we submit that in course of time bovine horns, the outcome of the crescent, developed into a special mark of honour and dignity, which men adopted for their own distinction, as well as the symbol of the most potent protectors.

No less a writer than Coleridge (*Literary Remains*, vol. i. p. 120) says, "No one has yet discovered even a plausible origin for this symbolism as to horns"; but with all deference to so distinguished an author, it is at least suggested that what we have shown to be the distinguishing badge of the highest of the gods, may well have been adopted in times past as the peculiar sign applicable to mark those among men entitled to great distinction. Reflecting, too, that even Roman emperors were deified after their death, it is going but little further to maintain that godlike symbols were applied to them while still living. The real difficulty, which we cannot get over with certainty, is how a badge, which at first appears to have denoted a female, came to be applied to males as well; moreover, as time went on, we find in later Roman days, the symbol when applied to a female, reverted to the primitive crescent, while the development of the horned moon, which had grown into the resemblance of the natural horns of various animals, became applied exclusively to males. It may be remarked, however, that inasmuch as very many of the symbols of classic times came from Egypt, and that the cow had become that of Isis in her form Hathor, so we know that the bulls Apis and Mnevis represented her consort, the supreme god Osiris; and therefore we may take it that on male personages horns typify Osiris, or the sun, while on females they refer to Isis, or the moon. Allowing, too, for the confusion which seems to be inseparable from all mythologies, we see how at least the idea came to Greece and Rome which led to their placing horns upon the head of Zeus-Jupiter, as well as the thunderbolt in his hand. [This idea fails to take into account the fact that horned animals and deities were important elements of southern European culture prior to contact with Egypt.] In

The Dawn of Civilisation, pp. 662–3, we see first Ramman, the great god of the Chaldeans, depicted as holding an axe in his hand, while over his head are his symbols, the sun and moon, which seem to have both been attributed to him, inasmuch as we are told that he had acquired in popular belief the powers of both the gods, whom they once separably represented.

Next we see Ramman with the axe in one hand, and the thunderbolt, evidently the same as the classic,[6] in the other, while on his head are two pairs of horns, which again we will conclude to represent the double powers assumed, just as in later times the typical double crown represented rule over upper and lower Egypt. We venture to pursue the analogy further, and to point out that the triple crown always given to the Pope is but the outcome of the self-same idea.

Isis was commonly depicted with the long horns of an Egyptian cow, so also was she in her Greek form Hera; and while the Roman Diana had gone back to the undeveloped crescent, so has her direct descendant still regnant. Hermes (Mercury) is said to have placed cow's horns upon the head of Isis, and thereby we can see the close connection between her and the sacred cow of the East, which having swum across the Bosporus (the passage of the cow) became Iö or Hera, the moon goddess of the Greeks. We learn from good authorities, both ancient and modern, that the cow horns of Iö-Hera were derived from the symbolic horns of the crescent moon, and left her badge upon Byzantium, the same crescent which still distinguishes the conquering Turk. The unchallenged assumption among all the Latin races that the moon is feminine and the sun masculine, has not been always so. Among Teutonic people we find a trace of their descent from a different stock by their usance in this particular. Modern Germans, it must be remembered, speak of *die Sonne* and *der Mond,* while curiously we find the same genders ascribed to each among the Australian aborigines. We may remark in passing, that a coincidence in people so far separated may fairly be said to be one of those minor facts which go to support the evidence of a common ancestry. In any case it proves that in primitive days people did not all think the moon a woman, or that the crescent was suitable only for female wear.[7] Even among the Egyptians this was certainly the case, for we find several male deities, such as *Thoth* and *Chonsu,* wearing the crescent as a crest. Further, one of the very oldest of the gods, *Chnemu,* the "Moulder," is represented with the head of a ram, having very distinct ram's horns on the side of his head, while besides these he has wide-spreading cow's horns as part of his very elaborate crest.

Thus we repeat as to horns in very early days, that those of the moon developed into cows' upon females and the horns of the bull Apis upon males; while those of the ram, the symbol of prolific paternity, were placed in addition as distinctive marks upon the heads of the greatest and most powerful of the deities. In support of this contention, as against the suggestion that the converse may have been the case and that the bull's horns may first have been placed on man's head as in the Minotaur, we would point to the very archaic figures discovered at Mycenae. Several are shared in Schliemann's book.

These are undoubtedly female figures, and the crescent instead of being on the head is the body itself, from which the neck and head rise up, thus indicating that the entire figure is a personification of the moon. Other figures of the same kind (of which the writer possesses one found in Cyprus) have the body circular, thus representing the moon, still unmistakably female, at the full.

Whether the moon's horns were first placed on male or female gods, very little affects the main question under discussion.

The confusions in mythology are infinite.

It seems, then, easy to understand how, as before suggested, that horns, the symbols which we have shown to denote the highest power and dignity in the gods, came in course of time to be looked upon as suitable for a mark of honour also upon victorious man.

Our head of Jupiter (Fig. 3) is from an ancient gem, and may be fairly taken as a typical representation of the god. Many examples exist of Roman engraving, which, though slightly differing, are almost identical in general design, and although we might begin much earlier, yet for our purpose this will be a convenient starting-point. Every object on the head has its distinct and well-known meaning. The corn measure of Serapis, the horn of Ammon, the rays of Phoebus, show him

Fig. 3.

to combine in his own person the powers of all three. Each of these attributes represents the sun god at a different season of the year.

The corn measure or *modius* is often called the *Calathus* or flower-basket, but the idea of ripe vegetation is the same in both. It is placed on his head as the type of the highest of his benefits, and is said by Macrobius to represent "the height of the planet above us and his all-powerful capaciousness, since unto him all things earthly return, being drawn up by the heat that he emits."

The god's own description of himself to Nitocreon, king of Cyprus, was—

"A god I am, such as I show to thee,

The starry heavens my head, my trunk the sea;

Earth forms my feet, mine ears the air supplies,

The sun's far-darting brilliant rays mine eyes."[8]

The darting rays are nearly always present in these portraits of the king of the gods; and in them we cannot fail to see not merely the germ but the fact, and hence the significance of the many upright points always shown on the typical crown upon the head of King David in Scripture story books. [It is noteworthy that the Pagan statues of the woodland god Silvanus depict him with a crown bearing spikes of some kind, although he is not associated with the celestial.] What we mean is well marked in the simple crowns given to the Magi at the Epiphany. Of these we reproduce two illustrations by two old masters (Figs. 4, 5), from Rosini, *Storia della Pittura Italiana.*

Again we see the same simple crown made up of spear-shaped rays upon the head of the Virgin Mother in a lovely picture of the older Umbrian school. (Fig. 6.) We have to refer again to this illustration later on. The rays and horn combined on Jupiter (Fig. 3) explain to us likewise the meaning of the erect *panache* upon the knight and Indian chief, of whom we have yet to speak.

Jupiter Serapis is nearly always represented on coins and gems with the curled horns of Ammon, reminding us very much of the spiral gold ornaments worn to-day by Dutch peasant women, and obviously showing by their conventional curl whence the common fossil "ammonites" take their name.

Fig. 4. Andrea di Salerno, 1480. Rosini, v. 24.

Fig. 5. Lorenzo Monaco, Rosini, ii. p. 160.

Fig. 6. Mino Senese, 1287, from Rosini, *Storia della Pittura Italiana*,
vol. i, pl. 153.

As upon the gods of Egypt, so in many Roman statues we find horns upon the head of both male and female figures. Juno Sospita is twice represented by statues in the Vatican Museum with the skin and horns of a goat on her head, precisely in the same position as those of a bison, to be seen on many North American chiefs, such as Mahtawopah, or the Blackfoot Petoh-peekiss. (Figs. 7, 8.) Who will venture to deny that the same idea is typified in these examples of the goat and bison's horns worn as a head-dress, taken from two different hemispheres separated by so many centuries in time, and still more by so great a difference in civilisation? At Durban the Kaffir *rickshaw men* wear horns upon their heads.

Fig. 7. Mahtawopah, Catlin, vol. i. p. 146.

Fig. 8. Petoh-peekiss, Blackfoot, Catlin, vol. i. p. 14.

Montfaucon gives two Muses horned. Mercury is frequently shown with wings like horns on his head, but about these there is more to be said. On the one hand in Chapter IV., Mercury is shown distinctly horned. In another case he is shown with a crescent on his head between the wings, thus forming a sort of complex panoply reminding us much of Egyptian combinations. Diana appears repeatedly in the pages of Montfaucon with the crescent so posed as to appear like the horns of a cow.

Bacchus (Dionysos) is commonly shown with horns; indeed, Horace calls him 'Bicorniger.'

The writer possesses a terra-cotta head of Dionysos found at Taranto: on this may be seen two horns as of a young bull, very similar to those on Michael Angelo's Moses. This head was a pre-affix to the beam projecting from a Greek house, on which we have more to say later.

The cult of Dionysos was practised and held in the highest esteem at ancient Tarentum. The principal temple there was dedicated to him. In Chapter V., wherein we deal with a remarkable find at Taranto, Dionysos is very largely represented.

These facts are mentioned to prove the familiarity of people in classic times with the notion of human heads having, or seeming to have, horns growing on them.

The very frequent references in Scripture to the lifting up or to the cutting off of horns have, so far as the present writer is aware, been dealt with slightly and unsatisfactorily; while the very number of allusions to horns in the Scriptures, whether figurative or literal, testify to the importance of the subject.

Much has been written upon the horns which tradition gives to Moses. A very learned commentator gives a long list of authorities *Mosem cornutum exhibentes*, *i.e.*, showing him as actually horned; and upon the passage Deuteronomy xxxiii. 17, "His glory is like the firstling of his bullock,[9] and his horns like the horns of unicorns,"[10] he remarks, "*Cornu enim potentiae symbolum fuisse norunt omnes*" *i.e.*, all people have understood the horn to be the symbol of power.

The Israelites were, of course, quite familiar with horns upon the heads of the gods of Egypt, and fresh from the land of bondage they would readily believe that their great law-giver had become divine, that he had miraculously received the mark of divinity and of kingly power. The belief that Moses actually descended with solid horns upon his head was devoutly held, and has continued to be believed down to the Middle Ages. Even later, the learned Grotius says that the god Mnevis (always represented with horns),[11] who was worshipped among the Egyptians, is believed to be no other than Moses himself. Mnevis was the sacred bull of Heliopolis, as Apis was that of Memphis. Spannheim lends his great authority to this by quoting Grotius, and supports it by adding that Aben Esdra himself believed the same. He says, too, that St. Jerome held fast the belief in actual horns on the head of Moses, and he (Spannheim) makes his remarks seem all the more probable, in establishing what was the belief of the Israelites, by the production of numerous coins bearing horned heads both bearded and beardless. A Greek one of Agrina in Sicily has a horned head, here produced (Fig. 9) which may be either male or female, but looks most like a woman; another of Gela (Fig. 10) has an undoubted female face. On the reverse of both these coins is a minotaur, in each case almost precisely

Fig. 9. Spannheim.   Fig. 10. Gela.

like a large relief from Nimroud, called a "man-headed bull," to be seen in the British Museum, on the wall opposite to the great winged bulls. Another coin, almost identical, is given by Montfaucon (iii. 120). Yet another of Megara, alike in character, is given by Spannheim, and still another of Catania, by Mr. A. J. Evans, in Freeman's *Sicily*, vol. iv. Besides these we have abundant evidence of horned heads amongst the Greeks and Romans.

Fig. 11.

Fig. 11 represents two out of a procession of ancient Greek soldiers upon a fragment of a vase found at Mycenae. On these Schliemann remarks: "From the fore part of the helmet rises a long and very curious object, which forms a curve, and is much like a horn. It is altogether inexplicable to me what it can have been used for, and there is no record in Homer which might be interpreted so as to indicate its existence on the Homeric helmet." With all deference to so great an authority, it is submitted that we have abundant evidence of what it was. These figures are crudely drawn in profile, and except that the shield is smaller and differently shaped, we see almost the same soldier reproduced in Fig. 18, from Mr. Leaf's Homer. The single horn in profile is intended to represent the pair of horns shown on the front view. Probably this is indicated by the two lines by which each is depicted. This explanation is confirmed by a golden ornament found at the same place, representing two men (? soldiers), full-face, each having two horns on his head.

The Salii (Fig. 12), called also "Flamines martiales," priests of Mars, in ancient Rome, wore a very remarkable spike or horn upon their heads, which was called *apex*. It is suggestive of, and in some respects like, the favourite *pickel* upon the helmet of German and our own soldiers of to-day; and thus we prove the very self-same idea to have prevailed in both ancient and modern times.

Fig. 12. Salii from Montfaucon.

To show how very important this apex was considered, we are told that the Salii took great care lest by any chance their cap should fall from their head, and thereby their horn of office should be brought low, and so dishonoured. A certain Sulpitius was deprived of his priesthood because his apex fell from his head while performing his service.[12] The cap of the Flamines was called *albogalerus*; they always wore it, and were not permitted to leave the house without it. We note this single horn, though it seems to tell against the explanation of the single one shown on the Greek soldiers on the Mycenaean vase. We are, however, only concerned with facts, and must not omit those we cannot explain.

Returning to Moses, it has been said by various modern writers that it is absurd and ridiculous to represent him as in the famous statue by Michael Angelo (of which a copy is to be seen at South Kensington). We are told that the idea arose from the error of the Vulgate translators of Exodus xxxiv. 29, where it is stated: "*Quod cornuta esset facies sua ex consortio sermonis Domini.*" The A.V. is quite silent on this, but the R.V. has "horns" in the margin, and these are distinctly named in the Hebrew. "It came to pass . . . when he came down from the mount, that Moses wist not that the skin of his face *shone* while he talked with him." R.V. notes "*shone*=sent forth beams (Heb. horns)." Thus it is clear the Vulgate translation is not erroneous, but literal. Pignorius (a well-known mediaeval writer) says distinctly of Moses: "*Qui a congressu Domini Dei Exercituum faciem cornutam referebat.*"

There is thus considerable variation between the A.V. and the Vulgate, but whether or not the translation given in the latter be right or wrong, the words used are the strongest possible evidence that the Latin translators were perfectly familiar with the tradition; while the abundance of statues and coins in their day, which they must have known full well, would prevent the notion appearing at all strange to them, even supposing they did not themselves devoutly believe it. The whole question turns upon whether the horns were supposed to be a miraculous growth, or a decorative ornament of honour and of glory. Later we show how the horns of Moses grew upon the mediaeval mitre, and how they remain there in modern ritual to this day.

Calmet distinctly asserts that the horn, so often mentioned in the Scriptures, was the symbol of strength or power; and we can scarcely doubt but that the Jews so adopted it, and of course brought it with them from Egypt, where they had seen it upon the gods, both male and female. The expression: "All the horns of the wicked will I cut off; but the horns of the righteous shall be exalted," can hardly be called figurative in the light of our present knowledge as to the ancient notions of Eastern and Egyptian people. The many passages relating to exalting, cutting off, or breaking the horn refer to the same notion—that of doing honour or of degrading. Nor has the practice of exalting the horn by any means been confined to the Jews. Bishop Taylor, writing about 1796, says that he saw Sepoys in India wearing helmets of stout leather; they were oval, and nearly flat, like the trencher caps worn at our universities. In the centre rose a headpiece ornamented with feathers, etc., and on the front directly over the forehead was a steel horn, rising as it were from a short stem, and then assuming the form of one of our extinguishers. Remembering how ancient, how conservative are all Indian customs, we may well compare this with the horns of iron made by Zedekiah (I Kings xxii, 11). We seem also to have a very near approach in this description to the spike worn upon their leather cap by the Salii and Flamines of old, but still more is the pattern preserved in the *pickelhaube* of the German soldier.

Again Prince, the African traveller, speaking of a cavalcade of the governors of provinces, says that each one, upon a broad fillet on the forehead, wore a horn or conical piece of silver gilt about four inches long, much in the shape of a candle extinguisher. This was called the *kiru*, or horn, and is only worn in reviews or parades after victory, doubtless as a symbol of honour or triumph. Both of these descriptions as to extinguishers very strikingly remind one of

HORNS OF HONOR

the horned head-dress still worn, as the writer can testify, by the Jewesses of Tunis, much higher exalted on the matron than on the maid. So, too, the Druses of Lebanon, until recently, placed a horn upon the head of their women, longer or shorter, to mark the married who have borne children from the single or childless. Fig. 12a is from a photograph of one of these Druse women, bought by the writer in Beirut; illustrations are also given of them in Smith's *Dictionary of the Bible*, ed. 1863, p. 827, *s.v.* "Horn." These are mentioned by Thompson, *Land and the Book*, pp. 73, 74; but his remarks are not such as to add to our knowledge or to impress the reader with the author's accuracy. Judging from this book, one of the chief efforts of the missionary is to uproot ancient customs of all kinds, and to level up (?) all converts to their ideas of modern civilisation.

Fig. 12a. Druse Woman.

"Tu spem reducis mentibus anxiis,
Viresque et addis cornua pauperi."

HORACE, *ODES* III. XXI, 17.

This was precisely the intention of Hannah, when she gave thanks for her son, and said: "Mine horn is exalted in the Lord." (I

Samuel ii, 3). In considering the whole context of this remarkable passage we cannot fail to be struck with what follows: "My mouth is enlarged over mine enemies, because I rejoice in Thy salvation." The conjunction of "horn exalted," of "enemies" whom I dared not mock by the wide mouth when childless, and therefore unprotected, but "because I rejoice in (Thy) salvation" "I have no fear," is most marked. Only a certain kind of commentator would attempt to spiritualise this very literal thanksgiving of an Oriental mother for the greatest of honours proclaimed by the "horn exalted," and by the safety (salvation), for her and her offspring, against dreaded enemies, which its presence was devoutly believed to ensure.

Alexander the Great (BC 330) was called the "Two-horned," and we are told that "the most natural explanation of this title is obtained by assuming that one of the attributes of Amen-Rā has been applied to Alexander. As the legend makes Amen-Rā his father this assumption is a fair one. Darius III addressed Alexander: "Behold it has reached me that thou, the Two-horned, hast assumed the sovereignty over Greece without my order . . . I will march out against thee," etc., etc. Among the Arabs various opinions as to the meaning of the epithet exist. Some say that Alexander was called "Two-horned" because of his expeditions to the East and West, and others because he had two curls of hair like horns on his forehead. Others again have supposed that the title has nothing to do with Alexander, and say that it belongs by right to a very ancient king of Yaman.

We venture to think that neither of these explanations is the correct one, but that it is to be looked for much nearer home and in a much simpler method. We show later that part of the regular panoply of a Greek warrior in the Homeric age, long before Alexander, was a helmet with two tall horns, and we shall show later that these horns continued to be borne by Greeks, Romans, Celts, Saxons, and Italians, down to a comparatively recent period, at least as late as the fourteenth century; therefore calling Alexander the "Two-horned," we suggest, was merely the equivalent of "Greek soldier,"[13] for we may well assume that he would bear the distinctive national uniform, and the name therefore becomes just as simple as to call a modern English soldier a "redcoat." Throughout the legendary history above quoted, Alexander is spoken of as the "Two-horned." The helmets shown in the accompanying illustrations may well support the contention here advanced. Figs. 13, 14 are from the originals in the British Museum. They are Greco-Roman from Apulia, pronounced to be of the fourth century BC. Fig. 15 is from the Naples Museum, and Fig. 16 from the Louvre. In both places are more of the same sort, and all are probably of about the same age or a little later.

Fig. 13. (Left): Ruovo; Fig. 14. (Right): Apulia.

As a military adornment the nations of old, Etruscans, Greeks, Belgi, Saxons, all placed horns upon their helms, in token of victory or defiance. Not only do we know this from pictures and traditions, but we have the

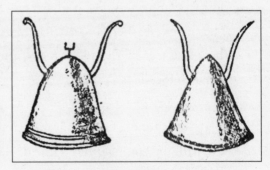

Figs. 15 and 16: Greek Helmets of Bronze.

very helmets themselves, and they may be seen to-day in the museums of the Louvre, of Naples, and of London, from whence our sketches

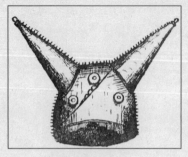

Fig. 17.

were respectively made. The small fork on some of these helmets reminds us that the ancients, like their modern descendants, were fond of piling up their adornments; these doubtless were to support the plume, the *panache* of heraldry, as shown on Figs. 18, 19. Even in England the horned helmet was worn. Fig. 17 is from the original in the British Museum. It is of copper, and said to be ancient British, found in the Thames.

Not only did the gods Chnemu and Osiris wear horns on their heads, but they are depicted with plumes upon them as well; the plume of Osiris is well known.

It may be here remarked that perhaps the plume rather than the horn in these modern days, and over a wider area, has become the badge of triumph, of honour, and of defiance upon the head of a warrior, whether he belongs to the Bersaglieri of Italy, the cavalry of Germany or France, the Highlanders of Scotland, or the field officers of England; but we have more to say on that point later on. The ancient feathers, indeed, are gone, but as may still be seen, upon these helmets of the old Greeks, the metal attachment for them remains. (See Figs. 13, 15.)

We give here a representation (Fig. 18), according to Mr. Leaf, of a Greek soldier of the Homeric period, in complete panoply of war, with the famous "round shield," which would be round if it were flattened out.[14] Here we see horns and plume as well. Comparison of this drawing with that of Mahtawopah (*ante*, Fig. 7) cannot but strike one with the strange analogy. Of a later date than this is the warrior from a sarcophagus (see Fig. 1) in the British Museum, from Clazomenae[15] in Asia Minor of about 650 BC. In addition to the horns, which are quite distinct—here, and on many of the figures depicted, we see the exaggerated crest or cockscomb before alluded to. The three lofty plumes forming the heraldic crest of our Prince of Wales are but a mere modern survival of an ancient object, and in the light of what we have yet to say on the subject of *panache* we submit that the modern plumes above the motto *Ich Dien* are a distinct survival of what is illustrated by Fig. 19 on page xx.

Fig. 18. Greek Warrior, from Leaf's Homer.

Almost every nation upon earth mounts a *cockade* of some kind upon the head of its fighting men. The soldiers of Magna Graecia, who wore the helmets depicted in Figs. 13–16 many centuries later than Homer, show us exactly what we would wish to describe, by merely supposing that each helmet had a central feather between the horns.

In Fig. 19 we have another of them fully equipped—the horns in a very pronounced shape upon the helmet, while between them rises what we now understand by a cockade—a stiff, upright *panache*. Even the most savage warriors, everywhere from Klondike east-

Fig. 19. Bul. Arch. Nap. Tav. XI.

ward to Kamtschatka, do up their hair into a sort of shock, erect upon the head, some-times mixed with feathers like our old friend Mahtawopah (Fig. 7), sometimes without; but we know the object itself to be but the complement, or the alternative of the horn of exaltation and of honour. The very cannibals, we were told by a traveller, place an object on their heads like a cockscomb.

The well-known *panache* of heraldry is but a name for a particular kind of crest, and curiously we find that in the days of chivalry *panache* got to be an alternative name for horns worn on the head, in fact a synonym.

Cotgrave translates *pennache de boeuf* as "a goodly pair of horns"; while Henry VI cried out at Ivry, "Si vos cornettes vous manquent, raliez-vous à mon panache blanc, vous le trouverez au chemin de la victoire, et de l'honneur." Again, a French apothegm says, "Quand l'hypocrisie a perdu le masque de la honte, elle arbore le panache de l'orgueil." All will readily admit the *orgueil* displayed in the elabo-rate *plumes* of heraldic blazonry, but what has here been adduced sufficiently proves that horns and the *panache* are really one and the same, in fact are synonymous both in idea, in origin, and in purpose, whether borne by knights, common soldiers, or by savages.

Abundant evidence on this point is to be found in Catlin's *North American Indians*, where we see many portraits of chiefs, some with horns, as in our illustrations, some with a crown-shaped *panache* of feathers, and some with a combination of both.

In support of this contention it should be here noted that in Italian *tromba* (trumpet) is but another name for a horn, when used in the sense of a musical wind instrument. It means also a cornucopia, and a ram's horn; hence, by a little extension, we can understand how the *ear* of Jupiter, as we are told, supplies the air; and thus a horn placed on the side of the head becomes a conventional symbol of his power over that element. At the same time it denotes his chief attributes—the sun in his might, as Aries the progenitor, and also as the bull Apis. We must never forget that his very surname, *Serapis*, perpetuates this Egyptian faith in a triune god, first brought to Rome by the Ptolemies, for it is but the contraction of the compound Osiris-Apis.

Having thus proved clearly that rays of the sun, horns, and the calathus, or corn measure, are distinctive symbols of the greatest and highest of pagan divinities, we now venture to maintain that in them we have the elements from which has been developed all the superstructure of that singular adornment, the modern crown of our kings—the distinguishing badge of regal power—and we hope to prove that it takes but little imagination to trace out each of these objects in that very remarkable head-dress. We do not here pretend either of these components to be the foundation, but that they are simply added symbols, piled up, as is commonly done, upon other objects, such as the Cimaruta of Naples, or the *Mano Pantea* and *Dischi Sacri* dealt with in Chapters IV. and V. However much it may vary in design, in general shape, or in material, we always find in the modern crown certain conventional peculiarities which preserve its main features. Whether, as it is said, crowns were invented by Janus or by Bacchus, there are remarkable family likenesses among them all.

In every example we have first a fillet or band by which it is made to fit the head, more or less ornamental according to fancy. This may fairly be said to represent the wreath or chaplet,[16] found alike upon statues of Diana of Ephesus, upon the winner of athletic games, upon the victorious general, and upon the eminent in civil worth. Indeed, corona (στεφανος) in itself signifies a circular band of metal, as well as a wreath of leaves or flowers; and thus we shall see that the name *crown*, which at first was merely that of the foundation, has developed at last into the term for the entire structure.

In classic days the chaplet, the crown proper, had various names, shapes, and materials, but all preserving the main idea of a circular adornment for the head. We venture here to summarise them. Among the Romans, the highest in dignity, the richest in honour, the most coveted, was the *corona obsidionalis*, made from the poorest of materials, such as grass, weeds, or wild flowers, and reserved for the general who had successfully relieved a beleaguered city. The *corona civica*, of oak leaves, was next in honour, and was the reward of the soldier who had saved the life of a Roman citizen in battle. Next were the *corona rostrata* and *corona navalis*, for him who had first boarded a hostile ship, and for the commander who destroyed a fleet, hence the *corona rostrata* was ornamented with a *rostrum*. The *corona muralis* belonged to him who first scaled the wall of a besieged city, and so the chaplet was battlemented; the *corona castrensis* to him who first forced entrance into the enemy's camp. *Corona triumphalis* was that of the triumphant general, while *corona ovalis*, of myrtle, was the reward of a merely successful commander. There was also the *corona oleagina*, of olive, for brave soldiers, which we may take to be the prototype of modern military decoration.[17]

Besides all these, the priests wore the *corona sacerdotalis* peculiar to their office. *Corona funebris* was a wreath placed upon the bier, not worn at all; whence, of course, our modern fashion, now at last so overdone as to become a nuisance, and hence a new fashion has arisen of advertising "no flowers" along with the notice of the death. The *corona nuptialis, convivialis, natalicia*, each denote their own object, and each had its own special materials, though all retaining the original wreath-like form. These latter, like the *corona funebris*, were not for personal wear, but were suspended over the doors as signs of mourning or festivity.[18] The extravagance to which the *corona funebris* may be carried is to be seen to-day in modern Italy. Huge structures in the shape of a horse-collar, made of palm branches, with flowers and other greenery, of eight or nine feet high, are borne along the streets, requiring always two, sometimes three men to carry them. One of these is hung up in front of the house for the very short time, before the dead is brought out; then, if not too enormous, it is laid on the top of an empty carriage following the hearse.

In royal crowns rising from the diadem or chaplet, that is the *corona* proper, we find many devices, all more or less as typical in meaning as they are various in design, but here again bearing evidence of inspiration from classic *corona*. In older crowns, such as are usually seen on the heads of kings of Israel (see Figs. 4, 5), there is a fringe of upright spikes, rising from the chaplet, which any candid

Fig. 20. Camillus and Brennus. Perino del Vaga,
Genosse School, c 1525.

Fig. 21. Raphael.

Fig. 22. Giotto.

witness will admit to perpetuate the rays on the head of Serapis. (See Fig. 3.) In Rosini's *Storia della Pittura Italiana*, Pisa, 1848, may be found a great variety of these crowns, as displayed in Art by the great masters of Italy, showing distinctly the features to which we refer. In one especially (vol. v. p. 192), in a picture by Perino del Vaga (Fig. 20), the king is represented wearing a crown composed of a simple band of metal, from which long spikes curve over the head. *En passant*, we call attention to the helmet of the general, which anyone can recognise as very like that now adorning P.-C. X. 248. Again, in vol. iv. p. 234, a picture by Raphael (Fig. 21), of "Joseph before Pharaoh," shows the king with a simple crown of the same kind, but with a ring of straight rays or spikes rising from the metal chaplet. The difference is that del Vaga makes his rays curve inwards so as surely to indicate not only rays but also horns, as we shall prove immediately. Compare these with the Virgin's crown in Fig. 6 and with the crown by Giotto (Fig. 22). The plain spear-shaped rays upon her head, in the picture by Mino Senese, have been conventionalised by Giotto and other masters into *fleurs de lis*, crosses, and similar fancies, but each of these fancy devices we can trace to its antetype in one or other of the various crowns of Rome that we have described, while yet preserving the general contour, and above all conserving the original idea of the sun's rays.

Next we find the curving, arching, bending objects in the conventional modern crown typified by del Vaga in the bending of the spikes, which can have no meaning at all in the form so familiar to us, unless they are a survival, and so represent the horns with which we are now dealing. In support of this contention, we produce an example that clearly shows what we mean, and is, moreover, modern of the modern. Fig. 22a is taken from Tenniel's famous cartoon, "Dropping the Pilot," published in *Punch*, March 29th, 1890, and reproduced in the *Pall Mall Magazine* for August, 1899. From Kaiser Wilhelm's crown proper rise six bent bands of metal,

Fig. 22a. Kaiser Wilhelm.

any pair of which fairly represents the pair of horns upon the Greek soldier (Fig. 19), or the helmet (Fig. 14). The rays on the chaplet are in their usual place, while each pair of horns is merely lengthened so as to meet in the centre to form a support for the supreme ornament, the ball and cross. Other good examples may be seen in the large cartoon by Sambourne, "The Roll of Fame, 1800-1900," published with *Punch's Almanack* for 1900. We submit, then, that these curving bands rising from the chaplet in our regal crown of to-day are proved to be horns, and therefore may be taken to signify the power and dignity of the wearer.

Lastly, we have the central ornament, of which there appears no sign in the previous illustrations until this last. It was often reduced to a mere button upon the velvet cap, especially in the crowns of the Middle Ages. Even here, however, we shall notice an indication of the horns (see Fig. 23). This central ornament, however, in later days grew, and assumed a new and more conspicuous form; it was the meeting-point of the arching horns, and it has at last, in our modern royal crown, grown and blossomed out from a bud or button into a full-blown orb and cross, like that on the head of the Kaiser (Fig. 22a), certainly a very suitable crest for the adornment of the royal head. In another place we have proved that this orb and cross are none other than the ancient *crux ansata*, the symbol of life to Egyptian kings, the astronomical sign of Venus Aphrodite, and a very potent protector against evil. The button finial of the sixteenth century, now in these latter days developed into the elaborate orb and cross, is, we maintain, no other than a survival of the calathus upon the head of Jupiter-Serapis, on which we have already remarked. Hence, reduced to its component elements, we repeat, a modern kingly crown is but the symbolic representative (possibly unintentional) of the ancient attributes of the king of gods. We even venture to go further and at least to suggest a reason for the development of the *calathus* into the more ornamental ball surmounted by the

Fig. 23. Rossini.

Maltese cross. In itself, the *crux anzata* is *par excellence* the cross of Amnion or Serapis; and thus its own proper place, as an attribute of his power, can surely be nowhere so fitting as to be set up for a terminal ornament on the modern crown of our ancient kings.

A signet of Francis I, Duke of Brittany, about 1444, bearing his effigy, represents him with a crown, above which two long ears project so as to give the appearance of horns, and yet these are by no means asses' ears. On the contrary, we shall produce evidence to show that they are curious links in the chain preserving the idea of the horn-like ears of Serapis, through the late Roman Mercury before mentioned, down to a quite comparatively recent period of chivalry, as the badge of a victorious ruler. We have seen other instances of ears so prolonged upon distinguished heads as to look like horns. So, too, we see plumes almost conventionalised into horns upon the head of Osiris and on the crest of the Prince of Wales; and further, we would point to the strange indentations in the bronze horns on Fig. 13, and suggest that therein we see an attempt to indicate feathers, and if this be so the identity of horns and *panache*, even in ancient days, is amply demonstrated.

To Italians, however, as the successors of the old Serapis worshippers, we must go for examples of the continued use of the horn of honour and exaltation in unmistakable plainness.

It is curious to find that among the many thousands of tourists who have visited the cathedral of San Gennaro at Naples, all have been so apparently wrapped up in the miracle of the liquefaction of the blood as never to have noticed what, to this writer, is by far the most interesting object in the whole building. No doubt it is thus neglected, because neither the Murrays, the Baedekers, the Hares, nor any other of the compilers of guide books have, so far as we know, ever had eyes to see it, for the reason that it is to them overshadowed by more attractive and popular objects.

One of the side chapels—that on the right of the high altar—belongs to the Minutoli family, and contains two pictures, said to be by Giotto in the guide books. There, of course, tourists flock to worship Giotto and Simone (Memmi) Senese, but no one has writ that the walls of the chapel are of far more historical value and interest than can be derived from two black little altar pictures, even though they may possibly be by Giotto himself. These walls are a history in themselves of Naples in the Middle Ages. On two sides the lower part of the walls of this chapel are covered "on the line" by a kind of procession of painted knights, nearly life-size and nearly full length. They end at about the knees.

The mural frescoes in this chapel which really lend to it its chief interest are said by the priest in charge, Padre Ruffo, to be by Tommaso degli Stefani,[19] who was born in 1230.

Of the knights, which at once attracted our attention, there are no less than twenty-one, all wearing approximately similar costumes, with flat, rounded helms, and all much of the same pattern, but with this difference, twelve out of the twenty-one bear a pair of horns such as are here depicted. The two figures here sketched (Figs. 24, 25) are consecutive, and may be taken as quite typical of the

Fig. 24 and Fig. 25.

whole; they were selected simply because they were in the best light. No photographs are to be procured, and even the rough sketch by the writer was obtained with some difficulty and after a little silver diplomacy.

The chapel is badly lighted, and it is probable that a vast majority of the visitors who enter it do not remain long enough to become accustomed to the gloom, and so never observe these remarkable wall frescoes on which the guide books are silent.

These twenty-one figures are described by the priest in charge of the chapel as personages of the very ancient family of the Minutoli, who had distinguished themselves in arms and in other virtues, of which the chief in this family was considered to be piety, and "hence each one is painted with his hands folded in the attitude of prayer." How ancient is the pose of hands in prayer may be read in Homer. "Loud prayed for them Chryses, lifting up his hands."

In the days of the Angevin and Aragonese lords of Naples, during the twelfth and thirteenth centuries, tournaments used to be held in the streets Incoronata, Carbonara, and Costantinopli, when each knight in turn presented himself at the sound of the tromba; and the herald, after having examined his title of nobility, proclaimed it to the assembled people, likewise by the sound of the trumpet, and thus introduced the jousters to the tournament.

A living historian remarks, "Neapolitans were not the morally and physically enfeebled race they now appear, until after the fatal admixture of the Spanish blood, or rather the Bourbon degradation. . . . Under their Angevin rulers they were a martial not a debased people." Again he says, "The tournament and the troubadour flourished in Naples, though not in Rome or Florence. . . . More virile surely were the warlike people who built St. Elmo and Castel Nuovo . . . and the first stages of the tower of Santa Chiara than their modern posterity." These were all built before 1300.

Upon the causes of the decline we can but offer a diffident opinion, but there is surely some ground for believing it to have had its beginning in the contests within the Church, which led to the "Great Schism" of the rival Popes Urban VI. and Clement VII. in 1377. We read that "all ecclesiastical powers and privileges were incorporated with the jurisprudence of the Kingdom of Naples, which, especially after the accession of the Angevin line, stood in a peculiar relation of dependence upon the Holy See." The Holy See itself had been removed to Avignon in 1305, and naturally its remoteness had exercised somewhat of a blight upon Naples during the seventy years of its undisputed reign in a foreign country; but when in 1377 Italy was divided in allegiance, and Naples with Sicily joined France, Spain, and Scotland in supporting Clement at Avignon, the loss of stimulant from the Papal court would be still more felt. It is therefore to be expected that the martial spirit of the Neapolitans would evaporate with the emigration of their leaders; while on the return of the Holy See in 1447 a new current had already set in, manners, spirit, and circumstances had changed.

The wearing on the head of the *trombe*, as in our illustrations Figs. 24, 25, in the form of horns is said by Padre Ruffo to represent that the knight had been victorious. All the Minutoli knights are represented with two horns or none, it is therefore to be presumed that those who do not bear them were vanquished in the tournament or were noncombatant knights. Each one bears the same escutcheon with the spotted leopard on his left arm.

The remarkable part which this painted chapel plays is that it pictorially interprets the very common Italian adage, "Tornare con le trombe nel sacco, o scornato," that is, "To come back with the horns in a bag, or deprived of horns." This phrase is translated in Baretti's dictionary "To come home with empty hands," in other words, unsuccessful, vanquished. Here we find a most conclusive proof of the way in which habits or customs, long become obsolete and forgotten, have yet preserved a record of their ancient importance, wrapped up in the history of the words once used to describe them. In these latter days, however, those special words have acquired a force and a meaning altogether foreign to that in which they were first applied; while if used now in their original sense they would convey no meaning at all to those who know nothing of the customs which gave rise to them. At first sight, and without context, our English word *scorn* seems to have no sort of connection with the wearing of horns on the helmet as a badge of victory, yet in the light thrown upon it by the portraits of these old Italian knights we see clearly what our own common word really means. *Scornare* in Italian still signifies to deprive of horns, but at the same time the modern Italian noun *scorno* has to-day acquired precisely the same significance as its synonym *scorn* has with us, that is, disgrace, infamy, shame; hence ignominy, extreme contempt. In the old French, also, we find that Cotgrave gives "Escorne—shame, disgrace, contempt, scorn"; and also "Escorné—ruined, defaced, disgraced, scorned." In modern French, however, although we have heard the word *écorné* in the sense of disgraced, it would appear from Littré that in losing the *s*, the word has dropped out of literature in the sense of general contempt; while, strangely, it has adopted and kept alive in France the same reference to contempt in respect of conjugal infidelity and marital disgrace, that from the Middle Ages onwards seems to have been associated with the wearing of horns by husbands in England, as well as in many other countries. Frequent allusions to this are found in Shakespeare, but still more so in the coarser dramatists of the sixteenth and seventeenth centuries, who made breaches of the seventh commandment their principal stock-in-trade for the construction of their plots. In modern French it seems that the survival of the *s* is only found in the word when alluding to this subject, for Littré's single notice of this specially disgraceful meaning under the heading *écorner* is, that those who receive "*éscorne*" *dans la marriage* are called *cornards*.

It is a curious lesson in the development of verbal significance to find such an absolute reversal of meaning as the present use of the word *scorn* displays. Not only is the object of the ancient custom of wearing horns completely changed from honour to dishonour, but the word by which it was denoted has become entirely revolutionised. Further, we see that the sense of the word itself has completely passed over from the object to the subject. Scorn now signifies not simply disgrace or contempt, but the contempt felt by another for him who is disgraced or *scornato*—*i.e.*, dishorned—and by no means implies disgrace to him who feels the scorn.

That which we have shown to be part of the components of our royal crown, and even so late as the fourteenth century (the wearing of the horns on the head) to be the sign of honour, pride, and victory to all wearers, had become at the end of the sixteenth century, at least figuratively a sign of the utmost disgrace, and a mark of the grossest form of ignominy upon him who wore them. So entirely had this notion of turpitude supplanted all ideas of honour, that *cornutes* and the allusions conveyed by the word, became the staple commodity on which the Jacobean drama, and that of the Restoration, as we have said, was chiefly composed. The transition of meaning both in word and custom took place (probably late) in the sixteenth century, and is plainly exhibited by Shakespeare, who in his day evidently understood both the honour and dishonour.

Jacques.　Which is he that killed the deer?

1st Lord.　Sir, it was I.

Jacques.　Let's present him to the duke, like a Roman conqueror; and it would do well to set the deer's horns upon his head for a branch of victory. Have you no song, forester, for this purpose?

2nd Lord.　Yes, sir.

Jacques.　Sing it; 'tis no matter how it be in tune, so it make noise enough.

All.　*"What shall he have that killed the deer?*
His leather skin, and horns to wear.
Take thou no scorn, to wear the horn
It was a crest ere thou wast born:
　　Thy father's father wore it,
　　And thy father bore it.
The horn, the horn, the lusty horn,
Is not a thing to laugh and scorn."

AS YOU LIKE IT, ACT IV. SC. 2.

"Let's write good angell on the devill's horne;
Tis not the devill's crest."

MEASURE FOR MEASURE, ACT II SC. 4, L. 16.

The turpitude attaching to the wearing of horns was perpetuated long into the present century; indeed among certain classes
it may be said still to survive. A fair held at Charlton in Kent on
St. Luke's day (October 18th) was called the Horn Fair so late at
least as 1825. On that day a procession, of which we have accounts
dating back to 1598, used to start from Cuckold's point near
Deptford, and march through Greenwich to Charlton. The riot-
ous mob composing it used to wear horns of different kinds upon
their heads; while, at the fair, rams' horns, gilded toys, and even
gingerbread in the shape of horns were sold. All kinds of licence
and indecency used to be practised on Blackheath, whence the
proverb, "all is fair at Horn Fair."

The custom is said to have arisen from the symbol of St. Luke—
a bull (see Chapter III); and possibly the disgraceful notions connected with horns, which seem to have arisen in the Elizabethan
period, may have led to or have been an excuse for the orgies practised. The custom is also said to have arisen from a grant made in
atonement for an adulterous wrong by King John.

Even to-day we see now and again in fairly respectable prints that
the allusion to horns in this sense is by no means forgotten, while,
of course among the lower classes, the whole notion remains in full
force and is daily expressed in the coarsest vernacular. In France, as we
should expect, it appears more frequently and openly as the basis of a
joke than in English prints; for instance, the coloured frontispiece of

a well-known comic paper represented two smart young ladies, with a cattle show in the background. The dialogue was:—

"Qa n'a pas l'air de l'interesser?
De bêtes à cornes? Oh ! lá lá . . .
J'ai déjà mon mari toute la journée à la maison."

Going back to Italy, so completely has the notion of marital disgrace, implied by the wearing of horns, supplanted the old one of chivalrous victory and honour, that even the mere gesture called the *mano cornuta*, when made in a particular and well-known manner, is considered to be the deepest insult one man can offer to another; no less than the implication that he wears horns. It is this insulting gesture, explained later, that is expressed in the common phrase *Far le corna a uno*. The same is understood by like expressions in French, English, Spanish, and German; but inasmuch as gesture plays so much larger a part in speech with Italians, and with Neapolitans especially, than it does with other people, so the phrase and what it describes has a more deadly meaning to them than it retains elsewhere. Even with us, "to make horns at one" is an expression still to be found in old dictionaries, and in society somewhat less than polite it would be well understood, though obsolete, fortunately, in literature.[20]

Whatever significance may attach to horns as decorative ornaments, expressive first of honour and later, as we have shown, of the utmost dishonour, yet another aspect was not only the earliest in point of time but by far the most important in the place they occupied.

It was as potent protectors against the ever dreaded evil glance that in all cases their great importance consisted; not only were horns worn upon the head as objects intended to terrify the enemy and to protect the wearer, but they were placed for the like purpose upon buildings and various inanimate objects. Figs. 26–29 represent what the writer saw and sketched over the doors of four consecutive houses on the Corso Vittorio Emmanuele, near the Gradini Grandi at Naples no longer ago than 1895. These must have been seen by thousands of English, for the steam tram passes along within a few feet, and he can testify to their having been there many years. In 1896, however, the houses had all changed occupants, and only the marks of the objects remained.

Figs. 26-29. Corso, Naples.

We have shown elsewhere that the horse-shoe here in England to be seen nailed on stable and other doors is no other than the crescent, now usually inverted, *i.e.* with the horns downwards, a position some-times to be seen in the moon itself, and considered a rain sign.

The Quarterly Reviewer of July, 1895, p. 212, throws some doubt upon the horse-shoe being the crescent, but only two days before reading that article the writer was told the following: "I knowed a farmer not very var herevrom, an' he 'ad terr'ble bad luck wi' 'is stock. He knowed they must be overlooked. Well, a neighbour told'n he could'n expect no other, zo long as he did keep the 'oss-shoe wrong zide up; 'n if he did mind to save his beast (plural *sic*) he must put'n upright, wi' the heels o' un up on end. Well, zo he tookt and he turned the 'oss-shoe t'other way up, and he never had'n a-got no bad luck arterwards."

This was said in all seriousness, but though it does not absolutely prove the identity of the crescent with the horse-shoe, it does show that there is a belief current as to the latter being most potent when fixed with the horns upwards.

The writer possesses Neapolitan charms which might pass for either a Turkish horse-shoe, or the conventional Turkish crescent, which is much more circular, with the points or horns brought more together than in the way usual in Murillo's pictures, as it is generally represented in Art, or as an astronomical sign. We take it that the horse-shoe was once habitually fixed heels up, but that as time went on the position came to be considered immaterial, and so it got to be hung, as it now is, in the way most easily contrived. It will be noticed in Fig. 27 that both hand and shoe are pointing downwards, while St. Luke (Chap. III) is making the same gesture with the hand pointing upwards. On the other hand the *Dextera Dei* in this position (called the *mano cornuta*), above the altar in the tomb of Galla Placidia at Ravenna, is pointing downwards. We submit that these facts establish the conclusion that the horns themselves and not their direction, were of the first importance, and that their position, whether pointing up or down, was secondary, though not to be disregarded.

Fig. 30 represents what in February, 1899, was to be seen over the doors of a grocer's and a butcher's shop in the same neighbourhood. Nearly every butcher in the unfashionable parts has a pair of horns over his door, usually

Fig. 30.

painted red, blue, and white. Passengers by steam tram to Pozzuoli may see a fine assortment of these things at Fuorigrotta.

The following advertisement from a Neapolitan paper is instructive:—

"CONTRO LA JETTATURA.

"*Corni, porta fortuna, elegante e grazioso articolo in ceramica fantasia, da appendere in salotti, ecc. Chi rimetterà cartolina vaglia di L1,20 ne ricevera due bene imballati in apposita Casetta. Trasporto a carico dei committenti. Commissioni e vaglia.*

"*C. Lopes e C., fuori Barriera Aretina. N. 62— Firenze.*"[21]

It should be noted that *corno* in Italian argot means *phallus*, and hence is the most powerful of prophylactics, especially *la corne torse*. We have remarked elsewhere that in modern Italy charms of all sorts and descriptions are called *un corno*.

How extremely ancient is the practice of setting up horns or other amulets for protection upon various buildings, particularly on dwelling-houses, or in rooms, as in the above advertisement, can be inferred with certainty, although perhaps few, except at Pompeii, are now actually remaining upon ancient edifices. From the nature of the material used, this must necessarily be the case; yet we occasionally come upon objects which certainly bear out our contention.

In ancient Greece so much was this the custom, that although none of these protecting amulets can have survived *in situ*, because the wood to which they were attached has perished, yet we have abundant evidence in the great number of terra-cotta amulets, of a special kind, still existing. These, indeed, are so numerous as to have acquired a technical name of their own, well understood by all archaeologists—the pre-affix. They were all of a somewhat conventional horse-shoe shape, having a rounded socket at the back by which they were fixed to the ends of the horizontal beams or

Fig. 31.

HORNS OF HONOR

poles, supporting the flat roofs of Greek houses. These poles rested on the walls, and their ends projected so that the pre-affix formed a sort of finial. We call attention to the close analogy between these pre-affixes and the cross-finials described elsewhere, upon the roof poles of the Dubus in New Guinea. Nearly all the Greek affixes had a face of some deity or other in relief upon them, and so far remind us of the faces carved upon the ends of "labels" of fifteenth century Gothic windows. Plenty of them are to be seen in any museum of Greek antiquities. The present writer possesses several, one especially has the head of the Medusa of the early, hideous, split-tongued kind; another is an unmistakable Gorgoneion of the transition period (Fig. 31). It is of much interest to find this later type of face in the same place, and apparently of the same age, together with the archaic. The mode of dressing the hair is

Fig. 32.

the only thing in common with the early and well-known conventional head. But for the snakes this face might pass for any of the goddesses. Another of the writer's specimens is an unmistakable Dionysos—with two budding horns, like a young bull—the "Bacchus Bicorniger" to which we have before alluded. Another of these pre-affixes (Fig. 32) is evidently a goddess, perhaps Hera or Demeter, with a face of an altogether different type, and showing considerable artistic beauty and taste.

These two may be taken as very fair samples of the Greek pre-affix to be seen in most museums, and in themselves throw a bright light upon the original intention of faces we see carved over doors and on the outsides of buildings of all ages down to this present. Four others, however, in the writer's possession are of a totally different kind—a kind that if not quite new to most readers has not yet been adequately studied or defined. There is a single specimen of pre-affix in the British Museum of the same type, and we have noted two others in the Louvre, bearing distinctly female faces with horns something like these; but with these exceptions we have seen none others at all like them elsewhere. There are certainly none in the museums of Rome, Naples, Florence, or Athens, and we sincerely hope the beautiful drawings here reproduced may lead to discussion and ultimate decision as to whom they represent and under what attribute.

Fig. 33 is on the whole the most perfect of our specimens, indeed the most perfect we have ever yet seen, and shows more of the typical shape of the pre-affix than either of the others. At first we took it for granted that one and all of them must be Medusae, with horns mounted by way of reinforcement to the power of the head itself,

Fig. 33.

particularly as we bore in mind many undoubted gorgons' heads with horns upon them, with which we have dealt elsewhere.

Another of these heads is here given (Fig. 34 on page 52), having much the same type of face as the last, yet of course quite distinct and bearing its own individuality.

A third example is shown in Fig. 35 (on page 52), again alike, and yet again quite different. The points in common are the horns on each, and the remarkable expression of terror or fright which all three seem to have, and which is perhaps still more striking in the originals than in the drawings.

Fig. 34.

Fig. 35.

HORNS OF HONOR

Fig. 36.

The fourth of these strange countenances is altogether different. Fig. 36 is quite another kind of face, and is similar in type to general African features. Moreover, it does not by any means show that expression of extreme nervous tension so noticeable in the other three. Who can they represent? One other point beside the horns is common to them all—every one has distinctly pointed ears. That is a feature certainly not found upon the usual gorgon's head; neither is there on these heads very distinctly marked the usual snake-like hair, though we suggest it may be said to be indicated.

Two of these heads (Figs. 33, 34) the writer exhibited to the Society of Antiquaries, where he hoped to obtain some expert opinion upon them, but was disappointed. Recently he has shown all four heads to the authorities at the British Museum, and there he heard the opinion that they all represented Pan, proved by the pointed ears and by the hair, etc.

Without venturing to question so expert and decided a verdict, we venture to point out that only one of the four faces bears an expression at all consistent with that of the jovial, mirthful Pan, and that, except the ears, there is nothing to suggest that he is thereby portrayed. That the Medusa was often depicted with horns we have stated elsewhere, and especially is this proved by an antique bust of one of the Roman emperors in the Doria Gallery, Rome. Of the head on this bust we gave a rough sketch in *The Evil Eye*, p. 198, which is unmistakably a Gorgoneion. Further, this very Medusa has distinctly pointed ears. We also pointed out in dealing with this question how horns and wings seemed to have become almost identical upon Medusae, just as we have shown them to have been upon Mercury, and later upon the head of Francis I, Duke of Brittany. The same notion came down into mediaeval heraldry, when the *panache* was either horns or plumes indifferently. We also refer the reader to the Medusa on the cognisance of Trinacria (Sicily) in the *Evil Eye*, p. 292. It will be seen that wings are substituted for ears, while two snakes are so arranged on the head as to have the appearance and to prove the intention of horns.

Again, it seems to us that each face is distinctly female in feature, whereas we cannot recall Pan with any but a decidedly masculine face, however goat-like it may have been.

Moreover, it was quite usual to ornament other female heads with distinct horns. For example, Montfaucon, Vol. I., Pl. 31, Nos. 4, 5, shows two Muses with conspicuous horns on their heads. Again, in the same volume (Pl. 44, 45, etc.), Diana is shown with the crescent on her head, so drawn as evidently to make plain the artist's intention to indicate horns. Also, in the same volume (Pl. 13), Juno is twice represented with horns on her head.

On the whole, we cannot give up our first belief that, after all, the horror of the countenance denotes the Medusa; while as to the pointed ears and the horns, we have proved that she has been adorned with both. Moreover, both snakes and the snaky hair are often omitted, and we suggest that in ancient Tarentum, where alone these pre-affix heads have been found, the artists gave the faces pointed ears as appropriate to the horn-bearing heads they were moulding, and so perhaps set a fashion that came down to Roman times. Our contention that these are Medusae has the support of a very high authority. Mr. Marindin writes: "I certainly agree with you that the type of face suggests Medusa, not Pan. If you know undoubted Medusae with horns, that would suffice." We have therefore called attention to what we stated long before these heads came to light, and think we may venture to say Q.E.D.

We show later how, in course of time, terra-cotta objects were supplanted by bronze, so now we point to Fig. 37 on page 56, which is a sketch of a bronze boss found at Pompeii. It was once, like many others to be seen to-day at Naples, affixed to the outer door of one of the grander houses, and one cannot fail to notice what a very composite design is here also embodied. We may surmise that the owner had seen service in Africa, typified by the elephantine trunk and ears. At the same time it expresses the owner's worship of Isis (so prevalent at Pompeii) by the disposition of the elephant's tusks, so as to appear like the horns appropriate to that deity, raised above the female head, which we may take to represent that goddess. Besides this, the leaves and corn on the brow betoken the cult of Ceres also, or perhaps of more than one other divinity. The prominence, however, given to the horns in the device seems unquestionably to denote that they had been "raised up" on the house for horns of safety or protection.

Fig. 37.

Of much earlier date, is to be seen in the Museum at Taranto, a solid terra-cotta horn, life size, with a hole at the root-end for suspension. The horn in Fig. 30, to be seen to-day in many parts of modern Naples, is a very fair representation of its artificial prototype, known to be of Greco-Roman origin, dated not later than 300 BC.

The Etruscans, said to be the most ancient people of whom we have any preserved records in Europe, were evidently, like most primaeval races, strong believers in a future state, and took great pains to protect their dead; we may even suggest that precaution, lest the dread fascination should injure the bodies of their helpless departed, may have led to burning them, and thus we arrive at the ultimate origin of cremation, certainly not the earliest method of disposal of the dead. But we find that along with the burning, infinite care was always taken to preserve and to protect the ashes, in fact it equalled that taken by Egyptians to preserve and protect the entire body. Lest even these ashes should fall under the malignant spell of fascinators, they placed them in little urns of pottery, made doubtless in imitation of the hut dwellings in which they lived when alive, and there can be no doubt but that they were specially "designed to keep a ghostly evil eye from the dead." On these they placed the powerful protecting horns. There are many of these little cinerary hut-urns to be seen in the Etruscan Museum at Florence, and of these Fig. 38 represents a typical specimen, sketched from the original; and it will be noted that it bears no less than four pairs. There is no means of fixing any actual chronology with reference to these hut-urns, but we may at least form some idea.

Fig. 38.

First, they all belong to the early Bronze Age, which in Italy implies an exceedingly remote period, inasmuch as from the intimate connection between those countries it must be judged from an Egyptian standpoint; and consequently the Bronze Age of Italy is indefinitely earlier than works of the same stage of civilisation found in northern countries such as our own. In the Vatican Museum there are also several of these hut-urns, which were found on Monte Cavo, near Albano, under three distinct and separate lava streams. Now when we reflect that the summit of Monte Cavo was the goal of the Roman triumphs from their very beginnings, we may be certain that its history goes back very long before the foundation of Rome. It is in itself an extinct volcano, and must have been such for ages before then; for no account, even traditional, of an eruption remains. Yet it is evident that at some time or other there must have been three separate eruptions since they were deposited, so as to have spread three distinct layers of lava above the Etruscan ashes, once contained in the hut-urns now in the Vatican; and thus we are brought face to face with an extraordinarily remote antiquity.

Much later we find a Greek tomb in Lycia over the door of which were placed the protecting horns to guard in this case the bodies, not the ashes, of the dead.

Still later, when cremation had again become the fashion, we find many urns and other receptacles for the ashes, to be decorated with objects which were surely intended as protectors of that which they contained. In the Vatican and other museums of Italy are numbers of little marble house-like boxes bearing sepulchral inscriptions, and at the same time ornamented with erect serpents, a gorgoneion, or some other well-recognised symbol. Thus we see after an interval of unknown ages, from the time of the horned urns of the Etruscans (see Fig. 38), how, along with the revival of cremation, the same protective horns were placed over the ashes in the late Roman period, to which this belongs.

In Naples to-day most of the butchers' shops, as before remarked, have a pair of bullock's or ram's horns over the door, usually painted red and white. The fruiterers and grocers, indeed nearly all provision shops, as the present writer can testify, have somewhere or other the potent single horn suspended. This fact is remarked on by Canon Jorio, who speaks of them as being so placed. Even in this present year, 1899, we have seen many pairs of cows' horns fastened upon the top of garden gates. Moreover, a polished horn, or a pair mounted upright on a polished stand, is to-day a very common ornament in the hotels and in the halls of Neapolitan palaces.

In the Museum at Zurich is a remarkable amulet, said to be Pre-Roman. It was found "am Elersberg bei Andelfingen," and consists of a pair of artificial horns made of stone, and set up in crescent form, so as to be mounted upon a doorway or arch—precisely as is done to-day in various parts of Italy. We have remarked elsewhere on an ancient Greek cow's horn, of natural size, now in the Museum at Taranto, and it is of great interest to find the selfsame amulets, though not artificial ones, still in use, after a lapse of at least two thousand years.

Professor Haddon exhibited at the British Association at Dover some pictures of the *Dubus*, or large houses in New Guinea. At the end of each horizontal pole forming the main timbers of the roof were large branching roots, having the exact appearance of horns, and serving no purpose whatever, unless such as belongs to similar objects elsewhere. Although so striking to the present writer, he could not obtain any special information about them.

These things curiously call to mind the Greek pre-affixes to their beams, on which we have before remarked, and to which we again refer later.

We confidently submit that the fact is now sufficiently established that horns upon houses and tombs have existed for unknown ages, and that they still exist as protectors against unseen though not the less dreaded influences.

Thus far we have dealt with them as the symbols of powerful protecting deities; such they were considered to be, and they were used as a sort of silent and perpetual prayer for defence against the ever-present threatening danger. They continue to be so used, though the special gods once symbolised by them may be unknown or forgotten.

In the case of the Jewish phylacteries, originally amulets for the protection of the wearers, we know how they got to be "enlarged" so as to become a mark of Pharisaic honour and distinction. It is contended to be the same with regard to horns. First they were used as protective amulets, symbolical of the highest of the gods; and, bearing that aspect, they became in course of time badges of honour and distinction to their wearers. At the same time dishonour and disgrace were marked by the treatment accorded to them, whether that treatment took the form of exaltation or degradation in a literal or a figurative sense. Precisely the same feeling of honour or disgrace which used to belong to the wearing or deprivation of horns by an individual, is now transferred to and connected with the ensign of all nations; it is a badge of honour to be supported when flying defiantly, it is a badge of disgrace and of insult when trailing in the mud: hence treatment of the flag is either honourable or the reverse, both literally and figuratively.

The intimate connection between the protective and the dignifying quality of horns as a decoration is well illustrated by a piece of ritual which has lasted from early times down to these scientific, matter-of-fact days. In the Naples Museum is a great Assyrian bas-relief of a priest wearing a mitre, on which the two points are shaped into unmistakable horns, and it is of course well known that the two points of a Christian bishop's mitre, taken from the traditional head-dress of the Jewish high priest (see Fig. 39), typify horns, and thereby convert that headdress into a badge of power and dignity. In a Missal at Bologna of 1517 is another bearded bishop wearing a mitre, on which a very distinct white horn, painted upon a darker ground, springs from the forehead to the top of the mitre, where it forms the point.

Fig. 39. Andrea Sirani, c. 1600 Presentation. Rosini, vi, 75.

Perhaps not everybody is aware that the words still used in set-ting the mitre upon the head of a newly-consecrated bishop in the Roman Church are, "We set on the head of this Bishop, O Lord, Thy champion, the helmet of defence and of salvation, that with comely face and with his head armed with the horns of either Testament he may appear terrible to the gainsayers of the truth, and may become their vigorous assailant, through the abundant gift of Thy grace, who didst make the face of Thy servant Moses to shine after familiar con-verse with Thee, and didst adorn it with the resplendent horns of Thy brightness and Thy truth, and commandedst the mitre to be set on the head of Aaron, Thy high priest. Through," etc., etc.[22]

In the light of this modern rendering who shall doubt the verity of the mediaeval belief in the solid horns upon the head of Moses?

Here, then, we have both the scriptural ideas concerning a two-fold significance of horns worn on the head, expressed in the plain-est language and in the precise order in which we believe they arose. First, defence or protection, and hence their assurance of salvation or safety; next in their power and terror to the foe. When we com-pare this picture of solemn Christian ritual with that of the North American chiefs (Figs. 7, 8) in their war-paint and feathers, we can-not fail once more to be impressed with the perfect identity of idea underlying them all. "His head armed with the horns . . . . he may appear terrible." Surely this is more than a coincidence, and will scarcely be claimed as missionary influence in aboriginal America.

Having dealt elsewhere at sufficient length on the protective power believed to belong to horns in themselves, as amulets against fascination, it is unnecessary here to do more than allude to the use of them in connection with salvation taken in its true sense. In this connection we prefer to understand the word salvation in its more expressive form—safety. We find in 2 Samuel xxii. 3, "He is my shield, and the horn of my salvation"; in Psalm xviii. 2, "My buckler, and the horn of my salvation." Again, Zacharias said, "And hath raised up an horn of salvation for us." (Luke i. 69.)

It is quite clear that these passages all contain one and the same idea—that of safety through the protective power of the horn. The words of Zacharias, too, are curiously instructive by the addition of "raised up," thereby signifying the fixing up of the horn in the house of his servant David. Whether this means literally that a prophylactic amulet was set up over the door, as in modern Naples, or like a horse-shoe upon our own, we need not stop to discuss, for the object is immediately explained with the utmost clearness, "That we should be saved from our enemies, and from the hand of those that hate us."

We have selected the above quotations from the Scriptures because they are so accessible, and the most easily verified, and because they are obvious; but there are many other expressions to be obtained from the same source which show clearly, though less obviously, how strong was the belief in the horn as means of protection against danger.

The expressions in Isaiah lix. 17, "For he put an helmet of salvation upon his head"; in Ephesians vi. 17, "Take the helmet of salvation"; and in I Thessalonians v. 8, "And for an helmet, the hope of salvation," although figurative are none the less conclusive as to the current belief that safety from unseen and intangible danger, as distinguished from actual and violent attack, was to be obtained by wearing a particular head-dress called here a helmet. This is proved by the fact that the shield is in most cases mentioned as well as the helmet, *e.g.* in Ephesians vi. 17. The shield would guard against the fiery darts or the open attacks of the enemy, but against the unseen, insidious, more dreaded, fatal glance, safety could be found only in the wearing of the helmet. This of course leads us to inquire what sort of helmet and in answering this question we must again refer to the close connection between the symbol of honour and of safety.

We have seen that ancient helmets were very commonly adorned with one or more horns standing up upon them, sometimes without other ornament sometimes accompanied with wings, sometimes with the *panache*, which is really the same thing, being merely feathers in another form. Further, we have seen that the *panache* and horns were synonymous.

In Figs. 18, 19 we have shown the entire panoply of a Greek soldier of the Greco-Roman period, and in Figs. 13–16 the very same kind of helmet with which St. Paul must have been perfectly acquainted, and so used it to illustrate his discourse. It was, of course, that most familiar to the Ephesians, to whom he was speaking. We therefore assert with all confidence that the "helmet of salvation," or the "helmet, the hope of salvation," meant not merely the leather or metal cap, but more particularly the protective horns—the "horns of safety"—mounted upon it. This, we maintain, was the original meaning and intention of the horns upon helmets. They were first used as symbols of gods for protective amulets, then they grew to be badges of dignity, power, and victory, and thus their threefold significance is to be understood, whether worn throughout the ages as an apex by Salii, a mitre by high priests and bishops, upon the helmet of a Greek soldier of Ephesus in the time of St. Paul, upon the head of Neapolitan knights in the Middle Ages, or upon American Indian chiefs in our own day.

CHAPTER II.

HORNS OF THE DEVIL

HITHERTO WE HAVE DEALT with horns as symbols of honour, of dishonour, and of safety, but no study of this subject could pretend to be inclusive which failed to notice the popular notions of the personal appearance of the devil, in his special aspect of "Old Horny himself." [This is an interesting choice of words for Elworthy as this title is also commonly attributed to the Horned God of the woods in some systems of traditional Witchcraft.] It of course goes without saying that we have nothing to do with Satan or his sorrows, which have been of late the subject of a popular novel and play. This latter is the ideal personage created by the fertile brain of Milton, and belongs to quite a different sphere from him whom the people call the Devil. Our purpose is simply to inquire how the popular idea shapes him and how the image has grown up; particularly are we concerned with the prevalent vulgar belief as to his bodily appearance, so well described by Browning in the following:—

> "Note, that the climax and the crown of things
> Invariably is, the devil appears himself,
> Armed and accoutred, horns and hoofs and tail."

It seems to be quite a modern development of scepticism that has led to so much controversy about the existence of a personal devil, and hence we find several books of recent date, written specially to maintain his individuality, against those who argue that he is a mere principle of evil personified, like Siva, the destroyer. [The nineteenth century was notable for the "intellectual" assessment, which tended to be dismissive toward the beliefs of others in terms of how they regarded spirits and deities.]

Of these latter writers, unquestionably the ablest and the most consistent is Gustav Roskoff, whose *Geschichte des Teufels* (Leipzig, 1869) treats the subject in the exhaustive German method, tracing the belief in a personal devil to the primaeval dualism existing in the minds of all primitive people. He produces evidence of this from the Mexican Tetz Katlipoka and his brother Huitzilopotchli. The former is Lord of heaven and earth, above all the other creators, the sustainer of the world. The other is the negative principle—the destructive, hideous (*schrechlich*) war-god. The same notion prevails among several North American tribes.

The Esquimaux have a good god Ukuma, and an evil one Uikan—the raiser of storms and doer of all mischief.

Roskoff goes in much detail through all the old world tribes— Tungusen, Buräten, Ostiaken, nomads from the Black and Caspian Seas to the Siberian coast and the frontiers of China; also Beduinen, tropical nomads, and all the black races, showing the same belief; and all this with much learning and many references. He then follows up the same reasoning, and produces evidences of the like belief from ancient civilisation, discusses Satan of the Old Testament, points out that he is first spoken of as διάβολος in Wisdom ii, 24: "Nevertheless through envy of the devil came death into the world." [**The Book of Wisdom is found in the Catholic Bible but not in the King James version.**] Hence Satan and death became synonymous. Later the notion of many demons arose,[23] of whom the being known by us as the devil was chief. He it is who is called Asmodeus in Tobit iii. 8. [**The Book of Tobit belongs to what is called the Apocryphal Books of the Bible, which were all rejected for inclusion in what came to be the official Bible.**] Roskoff goes on to discuss the dualism also found in the New Testament;— the Talmud, the Kabala, and the Christian Church of the first four centuries.

He says that the full description, *i.e.*, details of the devil's appearance (*vollige ausbildung*) grew up from the eighth to the fourteenth centuries AD, and that the article of renunciation of the devil and all his works dates from the close of the Synod of Leptina (Listinense) AD 743. He gives, too, the early German form of abjuration of heathendom, including the three highest of the gods—Wôtan (Odin), Thunar (Thorr), and Fro (Sasnôt), and their *Gefolge* (followers, retinue).

He next deals with the period from 1300 to the famous bull of Innocent VIII., which marks the climax of superstition in the fifteenth century; this he calls *eigentliche Teufels periode*.

The second volume is devoted to the consideration and exposition of the witchcraft and enchantments [allegedly] practised in connection with devil belief and worship, on which we have more to say; but no one can afford to neglect Roskoff, who studies this interesting question, and without expressing any opinion upon his general purpose or conclusions, we most strongly recommend the book as an able and exhaustive treatise from his own point of view. His work has been taken as a text-book by others for proving the non-existence of a personal devil, especially Réville, of whose work only a translation has come in the writer's way. There exists, however, an enormous bibliography on the subject, showing the attention which has been given to the devil; a small selection only of such works as have come in our way are referred to in the text and footnotes.

As we have said, the Middle Ages saw the climax of belief in the devil, but the growth had been a gradual one and had been promoted by various causes, but perhaps chiefly by the materialistic teaching of the Church, with its fiery terrors, shown in such pictures and sculptures of the last judgment and the torments of the wicked, as were intended to work, and did work, upon the imagination and the fears of an ignorant people. Who that has seen such representations as the fearful frescoes of Orcagna in the Campo Santo at Pisa, or the reliefs on the west front of the Duomo at Orvieto, to say nothing of Michael Angelo's great fresco in the Sistine Chapel, can be surprised at the terror with which the evil one was thought of in the fourteenth and fifteenth centuries? Who can be surprised at the absurdly grotesque notions which popular belief associated with the hideous beings depicted for their edification with the arch-fiend at their head?

No doubt the imagination which created such objects as are to be seen in mediaeval art, had long been fed upon the older heathen notion of the mingling of human and animal forms, such as we see in the man-faced bulls of Assyria, the various animal-headed gods of Egypt, the centaurs, minotaurs, and the half goat, half man of the satyrs and fauns of classic times. We may see how this idea, probably received by the Greeks and Romans through Egypt from the East, grew and developed under the Gnostics, by the extraordinary combinations they invented, and preserved for our edification on their gems and other objects. From their queer fancies and remarkable combinations, the transition is easy to the monsters of the Middle Ages and on these, gruesome invention seems to have run riot, so that at last we see goblins and devils in all possible forms, made up of organic as well as inorganic objects, from a tortoise with a man's face and feet[24] to cooking pots with arms and legs, worthy of the caricatures in *Punch*. For instance, in a savage portrait of Alexander VI.[25] (Pope Roderic Borgia, dated 1545, just at the bitterest period of the Tudor repudiation of Rome) he is represented as a devil: one hand is made like a dragon's claws and the other holds a pitchfork instead of his staff or crozier; the face is monstrous, with an eagle-like nose; (*cf.* remarks *post*, p. 98, on the Indian devil at Naples) on his head is the tiara, but from the back of the head rise large horns. The figure is nude to the waist, and below that, the stomach shows the staring face of a lion, as if gaping and swallowing all below. A face on this part, *i.e.*, on the stomach, sometimes with the nose drawn out like an elephant's trunk, but much exaggerated and ending as a serpent, is a very common subject.[26]

All this pictorial fancy, however, was but the offspring of a firm and constant belief that beings of extraordinary shape were actually existent, and that they had been seen by persons of credit, even by fathers of the Church. St Augustine, while denying in words that demons possessed actual fleshly bodies, yet fully believed in their existence and that at times they became visible to mortal eyes. No doubt he was deeply impregnated with the materialism of pagan Greece, and his study of the Hebrew writers did but emphasise, or at most slightly modify, without by any means destroying, his conviction. We know, too, that his extreme asceticism would lead to a highly nervous condition, such as would be likely to enhance any hallucinations that a weak body might engender; and his dear friend Posidonius records that towards the end of his life St. Augustine's contests with devils greatly increased, and that he worked many miracles in exorcising them by his prayers. Indeed, it has been usual on this account to cite St. Augustine in support of the corporality of the devil.

St. Gregory ascribes the belief in visible demons to illusions caused by nervous disorders; but St. Jerome was a very firm believer in devils with bodies more or less human. Incubi and succubae were to him real beings, and he asserted that satyrs were not only real but that he had seen them. He looked upon them as coming from the lower world. He describes them as little men with curved nostrils, with the horns and feet of a goat. He says that one told him: "I am one of the deluded dwellers in this desert, who have imprudently offered a refuge to the incubi and succubae."

Not only St. Jerome, but later writers on magic, like Martin Delrio, Fromann, Torreblanca, and others, firmly believed in them. Even the pious Melanchthon, in many of his writings, has asserted the reality of Satanic apparitions, while Luther not only firmly believed in their bodily shape but distinctly supports Delrio and the rest in the assertion that they mixed carnally with human beings as well as with animals, and that creatures known as monsters were the result. Delrio strongly asserts this fact and it was confidently believed throughout the Middle Ages. Female demons, or succubae, were the constant tempters of both St. Jerome and St. Anthony; moreover it was fully believed that they were the common seducers of men, no less than that women had constant converse with incubi. Of the latter the stories are endless. Bodin declares that in 1459 a great number of honest women accused each other of having commerce with the devil, and that they were all burnt.

It was this universal belief in monsters as the offspring of human beings and devils, male and female, which led to, and was the subject of, the famous bull of Innocent VIII. (1484), addressed to the Christian bishops of Mayence, Cologne, Treves, Salzbourg, etc., against those who were guilty of such acts, whether men or women. It was this pope who commissioned the notorious Jacob Spranger to hunt out all such persons. Spranger was the author of a famous book, called *Malleus Maleficarum*, which subsequently became the very text-book of the Inquisition. In England arose the no less notorious Matthew Hopkins, the witch-finder, and we read that the staple accusation made by these wretches against their victims was that of being in compact with the devil. In all cases, as we show later in connection with the witches' Sabbath, the devil was held to have possessed himself of the bodies as well as the souls of those who obeyed him.

That this notion existed long prior to the fifteenth century, called by the Germans the period of the *Hexenverfolgung*, is proved by the belief that Merlin, the famous bard and sorcerer of King Arthur's court, was said to be the offspring of a Druidess who had been visited by an incubus.

Earlier still, Suidas declares that Apollonius of Tyana, who was credited with supernatural powers, was begotten by an incubus who came to and, in the form of her husband, deceived a newly-married daughter of that city. Servius Tullius was said to be the son of a slave by an incubus. Even Augustus himself was also said to have been so begotten. Torquemada, in the *Hexamerone*, relates that a girl of Cagliari fell in love with a young noble, but owing to her inferior rank was unable to meet and confide her secret to him. The devil, however, assumed the likeness of her lover, and thus possessed himself of her. On the other hand we read of a convent of Cistercian nuns, amongst whom was one whose blandishments seduced the *conversi* (lay-brethren), and who was declared to be a succuba, or *démone deguisée*.

Our old friend Delrio, from whom many of these stories are derived, maintains[27] that sorcerers and witches habitually consort with demons, and that sometimes there is issue between them. He quotes Plato, Philo, Josephus, Cyprian, Justin Martyr, Clemens Alexandrinus, Tertullian, and others, in support of his statements. He further contends that Genesis vi. 2 fully supports their assertions.

It was the universal belief in the Middle Ages that all sorcerers and witches were the offspring of these unhallowed connections, and also that monstrous births were produced from like causes. It is seriously alleged that one of these occurred at Schinin, and that the monster was about to be destroyed when the mother confessed to having been visited by *un lutin incube*.

Cecco d'Ascoli was burnt in 1327, on the Campo dei Fiori at Rome (where later Giordano Bruno also was burnt) for having had illicit intercourse with a succuba, or she-devil.

We learn, too, from Froissart that in 1386 a duel was fought between Jacques le Gris and Jean de Caroube, in consequence of the allegation that Caroube's wife had been visited by an incubus.

Hedelin asserts the existence of satyrs and other semi-bestial beings, and that there is *aptitude génératrice* between human beings and demons. He treats much of the qualities (*propriétés*) of the he-goat. He regards him as an *animal infect*. He calls special attention to the fact that it was a black goat which appeared to Count Cornoube, bearing on his back the soul of William Rufus *aux enfers*. In this we get a piece of evidence which shows that popular imagination made the devil black as early as the death of Rufus in 1100.

There appears to be in actual existence even now a tribe in the interior of Africa, called Wito, whose faces are of a type very similar to the satyrs of classic Art, but we do not perceive any mention of any growth that can be called horns. "Their foreheads are extraordinarily retreating, and the outer corners of their eyes and eyebrows slope upwards like those of the typical Mephistopheles; their sharp, aquiline noses curve over the upper lip like a beak, and their chins are prodigiously long. Their ears end in a point, like those of the ancient satyrs, and their hair, which they wear unplaited, is short and woolly. A more diabolical cast of countenance it would be hard to imagine."[28]

Curiously too, much light is thrown upon the question of what are now called gargoyles, by these investigations. We find that even the Chaldeans and Assyrians made use of images of monsters, *i.e.*, bestial men, to counteract the influence of evil spirits who were driven off by their hideous aspect.

Here we have the ancient form of the same belief which led to the carving in the Middle Ages of the "Devils of Notre Dame," and of the endless monstrosities upon our churches and towers, so that whenever we see a grinning goblin, like "the devil that looks over Lincoln," we are reminded of the days when our forefathers firmly believed in the things we have been discussing; so firmly, that numberless poor wretches were put to death after conviction by the testimony of their accusers, that they were guilty of the crimes implied by the term witchcraft, compared with which incantation, fascination, and enchantment were considered as but venial offences.

In all ages one of the prevalent ideas of the devil has been that of the "roaring lion, seeking whom he may devour," and he was believed especially to be lurking round churches; ever planning to destroy their towers or belfries with his lightnings and his tempests. From the earliest times the belief has existed of the antipathy of the lion for the cock, and while goblins in stone were carved and set up on the angles to scare off the rank and file, the arch fiend, the roaring lion, had to be met by the one creature he dreaded—the cock. Hence grew the practice of putting a cock upon the highest point of sacred and other buildings, so that when the bells were silent, the devil might always see his enemy on guard. To make the cock more conspicuous, he was first made to turn every way with the wind, so as to present his full form in every direction. Then, still further to make him so conspicuous that his enemy should not possibly elude him, he was gilded, and made to shine out brightly and defiantly. Hence the cock upon the steeple, always pointing in the direction of the wind, set the fashion of setting vanes on high places, while the preponderance of one special form adopted, gave the technical name to vanes of all sorts, the weathercock.

Who shall say that the hideous creations of savages, such as those of Sitka Sound, of the South Sea Islands, and the Eastern Archipelago, which we are pleased to call idols, are not really the outcome of this very belief; and that the worship paid to them may not truly represent the faith of the poor savage, that their terrible aspect will drive off the evil spirits whom he fears so much? He loves indeed the good ones, but he takes no pains to propitiate them, for he knows them to be always trying to help him.

We do not hesitate to assert this belief to exist in all countries in both hemispheres, whether savage or civilised; in China and Japan we know this to be so; in Shinto temples are abundance of monstrous images, avowedly for the sake of frightening off evil spirits. This is but once more reiterating the old story of how much more uncivilised (even perhaps civilised) man is moved by fear of what he dreads, than by love or gratitude to his benefactors.

Of course all the ideas and beliefs as to the genesis of demons on which we have been dwelling, cannot be separated from the kindred notion of possession, a form of belief which was firmly rooted at the time of our Lord, and has continued down to this day. [This statement is boldly used as though everyone in Western culture accepted Jesus Christ as their "Lord," which was not the case in the nineteenth century nor is it now.] Even in the writer's own recollection, a certain nonconformist divine, well known, whom he often used to see, professed to "cast out devils," moreover he was firmly believed in and was looked upon as a recognised exorcist. We have already referred to the assertion that St. Augustine was accustomed to perform the same miracle.

It has been generally held that the "possessed" were epileptics, and it is a curious fact in the history of surgery that the operation of trepanning was apparently first practised in Europe with the intention, and for the purpose of causing or permitting the demon, which was believed to inhabit the head, to come out. Professor Broca says that a certain Sehan Taxil published in 1603 a treatise on epilepsy, and in a chapter proving that demoniacs were epileptics he advocates the opening (*la trépanation*) of the skull, to cause the demon to come out. This notion was clearly both ancient and widespread, for the aboriginal inhabitants of Peru practised trepanning extensively. Numerous skulls have been discovered, on which the operation had been performed in a terribly rough manner.

Popular belief in the personality of demons could not but formulate some typical shape in which they ordinarily appeared to man, as they were believed to do, and our purpose is to ascertain what this shape was, and how it became established in the mind of the people.

The popular imagination from the dark ages onwards, has pictured the devil, *i.e.* the arch fiend, as a naked figure, half man and half goat, with a long tail, and always black; for this latter belief certainly still exists, and may well be said to survive in the common proverb: "The devil is not half so black as he is painted." The stories are endless wherein he shows himself in various disguises; but in nearly all cases where he appears in clothing, the horns, tail, or cloven foot are made to disclose themselves. On the other hand there must have existed in the public mind among the educated, long before Milton wrote his *Paradise Lost* (1652–3), a quite different conception of Satan, such as that to which he gave form and expression. This ideal was much higher than attached to the evil one in the commonly received notion, whom most of the writers down to the end of the sixteenth century had been accustomed to represent as essentially animal, both in form and instinct, whose chief, all-absorbing passion was lust, and whose human qualities were of the very lowest type. The popular idea of this being was such that he was always represented as the dupe, to be gulled and cheated by those he sought to make his victims. Stories without end exist as to his extreme gullibility and simple, childish want of perception; such histories as that of *Jack the Giant Killer* precisely illustrate what we mean, and the common phrase "cheating the devil" keeps alive the idea.

Alongside this popular notion of his simplicity and semi-animal shape, on which we have been speaking, there was, among the more educated, if not more enlightened persons, such as the monks and secular clergy, a firm belief in his personal malignity and high intellectual power, by which he was supposed to be always on the watch to entrap the souls of men. At the same time it is curious that Art should have followed the popular imagination and habitually have given him, as it did, the grossest, most bestial and grotesque forms, now leaning towards the scriptural serpent and dragon, now leaning to the black goat-man. In serious literature, from Genesis to Milton and Browning, he is treated always as a powerful though malignant person, endowed with great cunning and high intelligence. As a specimen, in one of the minor poems in the Vernon MSS.[29] of the fourteenth century is "A disputison between a god man and the dewel," in which he carries on an argument something like that in the Book of Job, and ascribing to him much cleverness and power of argument, but wherein the devil is always called either *false schrewe, wikked schrewe, wikked gost,* or *wikked fend.* He has always been held capable of assuming any form he pleased, and of showing himself to human eyes. In Milton's own time we find him in still more human and Miltonic form, assuming a mortal shape, and taking a very active part in worldly affairs. A curious little book of 1647 called *The Divell a Married Man,* though more serious and less of a caricature than Le Sage's well-known *Le Diable Boiteux,* is a skit upon matrimony, yet it paints the devil according to the then current belief among those educated enough to be able to read it. Even in this story peeps out in the end the common belief in the folly, and easily cheated character of the devil. Though a digression for which we apologise, it shows the prevailing notions in Puritan times as well as the *Sorrows of Satan* does in ours.

The following is an epitome: Belphagor, an Arch-divell (before his fall an Archangel), arrived in Florence and set up as a money-lender under the name of Roderigo of Castile. He made a great display of wealth gotten, as he said, at Aleppo, though he gave out that he was a Spaniard of mean parentage. In Florence he marries Honesta, daughter of a merchant, Amerigo Donati, but she proves such a fury that the other *divells* he had brought as servants, leave him, choosing rather to be free in hell than to live in a house with such a woman. His brother, whom Roderigo had established in business as a Levant merchant, gambles away his money, so that he is obliged to fly from his creditors, who closely pursue him. Roderigo is hidden by a bailiff in a dunghill, under a promise of great riches if he (the bailiff) will protect him from the creditors. When reminded of his promise he proclaims himself Belphagor, Prince of Hell, and that he will surely make good his word.

He told the bailiff he would shortly hear that a lady was possessed, and that he might be quite sure that he was in her; and, further, that he would only come out at his (the bailiff's) command. "You can make," he said, "your own conditions and thus pay yourself." A few days after, the daughter of Ambrogio Amadei was possessed. The ordinary relics of saints—the head of San Zenobio, the mantle of St. John Gualbert—were tried without effect, but these doings having come to the ears of John the Bailiff he went and undertook to cure her for 500 florins. Several masses were said, and some mock ceremonies were performed; then the bailiff whispered in the woman's ear, "Roderigo, be noble, be a man of thy word." "I will," quoth Roderigo, "and as soon as I am gone hence, I will enter into the daughter of the King of Naples, where also I will be at thy service." In a very short time it was noised abroad that the king's daughter was possessed, and soon after the king, having heard of his fame, sends for John the Bailiff, who makes a still better bargain, and with the same ceremonies as at first cures her also; but the "divell" before he departed said, "I am no more thy debtor, I am no longer Roderigo, but Belphagor, and will work thee all the mischief in my power."

John, who had received 50,000 ducats from the king, returned to Florence to enjoy his money, thinking Roderigo would not harm him. Soon after, however, he heard that the daughter of Louis VII. of France was demoniac, but John was so greatly afraid when he recollected the last words of Roderigo, that when he was sent for by the French king he pretended to be sick and quite unable to come. At last, being compelled by the Seignorie of Florence to go to Paris, he was brought into the lady's presence; but there he excused himself, and declared he had no power over certain "divells." The king, however, would not hearken to that, and in a rage replied, "Either cure her or thou shalt hang for it."

John tries Roderigo with entreaties, reminding him of how he had befriended him and saved him from his enemies; but the "divell" mocks and insults him, saying he will make him hang himself before he has done with him.

In despair John Matteo, the bailiff, at last thinks of another plan. He goes to the king and persuades him to have a great terrace or balcony made in the principal square of Paris, to have it hung round with arras, and magnificently decorated. Then he was to command the clergy to say mass; trumpets, timbrels, sackbuts, and all kinds of loud music to sound at a given signal; and that then, when the lady was brought out, the foul fiend would come out of her.

All this was done, but when Roderigo saw so great a concourse he wondered what it all meant; did John think to trick him? When the bailiff came near once more to entreat him to come out, the "divell" demands, "What is all this mummerie?"

The signal is then given, and the din of the music begins; upon which again the "divell" inquires what it is all about, when John in a great fright cries out, "Oh! Roderigo, it is thy wife; she is come to look after thee!"

No spell or enchantment so strong as this; at the very name of his wife he posts off to hell and leaves the lady free.

"Moral. No 'divells' will hereafter be valiant enough to adventure into the world to look for a wife. Unwelcome news this for many who are such she-'divells' that they can expect no husband but from hell."[30]

The *finale* of this story is quite in keeping with the old notion that great noise will drive away the devil. Bells in church towers were first placed there for that purpose, and they are the natural accompaniments of gargoyles, which are demons in stone; the one kind to terrify the eyes, and the other the ears, of evil spirits lurking about. At two adjoining parishes (the churches of both can be seen from the place where this is written), called Langford Budville and Thorne St.

Margaret, the bells of the former are (or used to be) rung on Midsummer night to drive the devil over to Thorne, and at Thorne the bells were rung on St. Margaret's Day to drive him back to Langford.

The story we have given above is another illustration of the simplicity and gullibility which, as we have remarked before, is part of the character popularly ascribed to the devil from the Middle Ages downwards, while at the same time it also shows that there existed a firm belief in his miraculous power.

The traditional idea of the stupidity and simplicity of giants, devils, and all superhuman beings, is no doubt a very ancient one. The story of Polyphemus, the giant whose one eye was blinded by Odysseus, and the more familiar one so closely connected with the foundation of Rome, how the giant Cacus stole the cattle of Hercules, and was afterwards outwitted and slain by the hero, are but myths upon which have grown up many legends of cheating or befooling the devil. There was no need of Ben Jonson's "The Devil is an Ass" to show his stupidity, a trait which was firmly established in the popular mind. He was, nevertheless, at the same time looked upon with the utmost dread, and this fear of the "evil one" has been stimulated, and much practised upon, by the clergy of all religions, down to the last, may we not say to the present, century, even to the present day?

We read of the Scotch Protestant clergy of the seventeenth century, that in preaching on the torments by evil spirits which awaited the sinner, they used language "calculated to madden men with fear and to drive them to the depths of despair." They told their hearers that they would be cast into great fires, to be roasted by devils, and hung up by their tongues, with other unutterable torments. The

Calvinistic preachers of the last century seemed, like the artists of earlier, and less lethargic days, to have drawn from their imaginations the most horribly realistic and hideous pictures of the devil and hell, for the purpose of terrifying their hearers; and they certainly succeeded in keeping alive in the popular mind the most fearful notions of the dread enemy, viewed from the religious side.[31] On the other hand, at the very same time there remained in full vigour all the grotesque and comic fancies, which no religious fervour and no amount of Board School education has even yet been able to uproot. Many of us still remember how our childhood was made miserable by our ignorant nurses, whose chief threat, and indeed actual punishment, used to be to put the child in the dark cupboard with the black man, or to declare that the old black man should have naughty children. These sayings and doings are undoubtedly the legacy left by our so-called pagan ancestors.

It would be a nice and an interesting investigation to determine which of the two parallel notions, the fearful or the humorous, now holds the firmest grasp on popular imagination. As a practical comment upon these two very opposite views of the arch-enemy, it is of some interest to look into the meaning and origin of the name devil, about which there are conflicting opinions. These have arisen, doubtless, through coincidence of sound. On the one hand, Grimm holds that the Teutonic words *devil, teufel, diuval, djöfull, djwful,* may all be traced back to the Zend *dev-,* and that our word is nothing but a corruption of *deva,* the Sanskrit word for God. This contention is supported by the fact that the Gypsies' name for God is *Dewel,* and that they are an Eastern race preserving Oriental names and customs. Dr. Tylor rather supports this theory, on the ground that Dewel is rather feared than loved by these weather-beaten out-casts, through His storms and tempests, and that therefore He is rather the author of evil than of good.

Dr. Murray (*H. E. D.*), does not even discuss this speculation, but affirms distinctly that the Teutonic *devil*, in all its forms, is immediately from the Greek διάβολος—accuser, calumniator, slanderer, traducer. He says, "The Gothic word was directly from Greek," and this we accept as final.

We hope to be able to prove that very distinct traces of both conceptions of the devil are to be seen in present-day representations of him. On the one side is the comical monster to be cajoled and cheated, the development of the old Polyphemus into the giant of the nursery; while on the other he is the astute, powerful Satan of *Paradise Lost.* The many authors who have tried to explain away his very existence we leave alone, inasmuch as they deal with a part of the subject with which we have little concern; we only have to deal with his personality as pictured in the minds of the people. We know that Luther thought he had fought out many actual contests with the devil, and that he devoutly believed not only in his individuality, but in his constant appearances in a bodily shape. The same may be said of John Knox, and other eminent divines, down to our own day. The writer has heard many local stories of his appearance and doings, which were said to have happened, quite within his own recollection. A cottage belonging to his father fell into decay, and has long been pulled down, because no one would live in it—"'twas that troublesome." A man of ill repute, well known to the writer, used to live in this cottage, but was accidentally killed, and current report said that "th' old fellow comed arter 'n." The next tenant was a man with a wooden leg, and he had not been there long before he came to the owner and declared he was "afeared to bide there, for th' old fellow, now that he'd a-had the old——," would not let him have any peace, for "every night he do come, and I do hear'n a-draggin' my leg all round the chimmer (bedroom) by the buckle straps."

Another case known to the writer, was that of a well-to-do man who was said to have "sold himself." He was always believed to be afraid to be out at night, for "the old fellow" had been seen by many people waiting for him near his house. He certainly never would return home alone at night; and this peculiarity, in an otherwise brave man, may have caused the story, but that it was firmly believed the writer can positively assert, for he knew him well, and the belief is all that concerns our present purpose.

We have already alluded to the notion that the devil is black, and that the idea proceeds from the primaeval belief that a black goat is at least half of him.[32] Popular notions, however, credit him with general lycanthropy in its broad sense, and not as confined to the wolf, though that animal has always been one of his favourite metamorphoses. Hence probably the cult of the wolf, so evident in Egypt at Assioot. The hare, the sow, and indeed every creature whose shape was assumed by the gods in classic days, has at one time or other had his body occupied by the devil.[33]

The hare was, singularly enough, an object of superstitious reverence and fear, in Europe, Asia, and America. The ancient Irish killed all the hares they found on May Day among their cattle, believing them to be witches, and therefore to have intimate relations with the devil. The same belief still survives in Somerset. Divine honours were paid to the hare in Mexico. Wabasso was changed into a white rabbit and canonised in that form. The Calmucks regarded the rabbit with fear and reverence.

The hare was unclean to the Jews according to Levitical law, but there has always been as much confusion between hares and rabbits as between frogs and toads, lizards and crocodiles; and also there is doubt as to whether the hare of Scripture is identical with the animal so called by us. We know that small charms with eyelets made like the hare were in Roman times protective amulets, and a hare appears very distinctly on the nail depicted in Fig. 159, *Evil Eye*.

Bochart deals at great length with this subject, and that the confusion between hare and rabbit exists to-day is proved by the following. "A sailor (South Devon) believed that if he said the word 'rabbit' at sea it would bring him bad luck; he always referred to them as 'the long-eared gentry,' and if I mentioned the forbidden word always expostulated, 'Don't 'ee, miss, please; you never know what mayn't happen.'"[34]

The exclamation "Drabbit!" is well known, and usually considered as a quasi-curse, like "drat it," but it is suggested that it may be an actual utterance by way of defiance of an unholy name. We have remarked elsewhere on the reluctance of fishermen generally to use the word hare, with the names of some other animals, and also as to words as well as acts of defiance against dreaded influences. The fear of hares or rabbits is doubtless connected with the belief in transformation, common to all systems of mythology, but in none is it more so than in that of the East, especially modern India. Much is said on this subject by Gubernatis in *Zoological Mythology*, two vols., 1872. He says the horn supposed to be on the head of the wild ass through the myth of the cornucopia connects the ass with Pan; and somewhere else we have read of a curious fact, which reminds us of the whispering to Roderigo in the ear of the woman possessed, implying that the devil resides in the ass and can be invoked by speaking in his ear. It seems that the bite of a scorpion could be so cured.

"Si quis graviter scorpione ictus, id in aurem insusurret asini, ex tempore curetur."[35]

Again we are told that the mythical centaur, the satyr, faun, ass, and goat are mythologically equivalent terms—hence "the devil is an ass" is quite a literal expression. Silenus is often represented in Montfaucon and elsewhere as riding upon an ass, for the ass was sacred to Bacchus and Priapus; he was moreover always present in the Dionysian processions at the Eleusinian mysteries, and thus a very close connection is shown to exist between the ass and Pan, the modern devil's prototype, as we shall show later on.

"Te senior turpi sequitur Silenus asello,
Turgida pampineis redimitus tempora satis,
Condita lascivi deducunt orgya mystae."[36]

In a monkish piece of wood-carving in the church of Corbeil, near Paris, is to be seen a practical example of the combination between the horns of the devil and the ears of the ass. Moreover we drew attention to long horn-like ears in chapter I, p. 35.

As regards this actual bodily shape in present popular imagination, we may remark that during the past few months the writer has met with figures of the devil in various metals and in various places, through all of which the same idea runs as that expressed by the poet, of "horns and hoofs and tail." From the back of a cab-horse in Naples comes by far the largest specimen; then in Rome a little oxidised silver charm beautifully chiselled; another of the same kind from Florence, but more roughly executed; while yet another is from Paris, where many are to be seen in the shop windows painted bright red.[37] The same Parisian model was recently for sale in Regent Street; therefore we are justified in assuming that these devils which are all alike in shape and gesture represent the popular notion at the present day. Fig. 40 represents fairly the general type, though it is really a modification of all four. The tail is leonine, and is copied from the Neapolitan cab-horse *diavolo*, whereas the horns on that example are distinctly bovine, and the face round, stupid, and clownish; the other examples all have sharp features and a cunning expression. The

Fig. 40.

attitude in all four is nearly the same. Curiously too, though coming from such widely different sources, and of such different models and sizes, all represent the same general features, and every one is in the act of performing the same gesture—commonly called "taking a sight" or "making a snook." This is the attitude of vulgar mockery among all people. Neapolitans call this *Besseggiare*, and it is given by

Jorio as one of their common gestures. Hence it may be assumed that the devil is looked upon generally as a contemptuous mocking personage, with a dash of vulgar humour. This conception agrees well with what we hope to prove to have been the character of his prototype upon whom the modern notion has grown up.

Having just bought the *diavolini* referred to, in Italy, on returning recently by way of the lakes, the writer was strangely impressed at Lugano by Luini's well-known great fresco of the crucifixion, where is to be seen above the cross of the impenitent thief the very common representation of the devil receiving the soul. The figure painted by Luini is still more suggestive of the grotesqueness of the modern representations. The difference is that modern art has deprived him of his wings, but this we can readily account for as we proceed; and meanwhile we remind the reader that one of our main purposes in the present study is to account for his horns; of these rather than his wings our modern popular belief takes most cognisance. In his name "Old Horny," and in that commonest of proverbs, "Talk of the Devil, and you see his horns," are evidently preserved at least one point in the people's notion of his outward appearance. [Here, **Elworthy somehow loses sight of the fact that images of the Devil came from agents of the Church, and that the physical appearance of the Devil was thereby introduced to the public. The Devil's visual form was never described in any detail, or even suggested, in any books of the Bible.**]

Perhaps to clear the way to the inquiry how and whence he got his horns in popular imagination, it is well to point out here, in addition to the facts we have dealt with in connection with the beliefs of the Middle Ages, that the popular notion of to-day is singularly at variance with that conveyed by Scripture. First we read of him as the tempter of our first parents, in the form of a serpent, and in that form he is cursed—"upon thy belly shalt thou go." [This statement represents Elworthy's belief in the Garden of Eden tale as historical rather than mythological. He also accepts the idea that all humans are descended from a single pair of people—Adam and Eve, whom he calls "our" first parents.] In mediaeval representations of the scene in the garden he is often painted as a serpent with a human face, for the old notion of lycanthropy, or transformation, always has attached to him. As before remarked, he was thought to be able to change himself so as to appear in any form he chose, even as an angel of light, and often in the shape of a beautiful woman called Lilith, as in the well-known picture of the temptation of St. Anthony.

In the Middle Ages, among other strange notions, there was a Jewish legend, very widely believed, that it was not Eve, but Lilith who seduced Adam, and then prevailed on him to eat the forbidden fruit, and that it was this unholy connection which brought death into the world. The serpent Apep of Egypt was the personification of darkness and of evil, which it was the business of Horus, the rising sun, to conquer and to kill, before he could appear in the east. In the *Book of the Dead* referred to later are found Apep, the Egyptian devil, in the form of a serpent and also of a crocodile, while an ass is shown in the serpent's power, thereby confirming by earlier evidence the connection, at least in idea, between the devil and the ass. There is no end to the stories in the Middle Ages relating to the devil, dating from about the time of the height of the belief in witchcraft, which latter was founded on the conviction of unholy compact with the devil; it was this that led to such fearful persecution of persons denounced as witches.

Many of these stories are utterly inconsistent with each other, and the student will find just as great confusion with regard to the infernal hierarchy as he will in classical mythology, where the same name represents many different attributes of one deity, and where many names represent the same personage.

In the Middle Ages the belief in witchcraft, or complicity with the devil, was a serious article of popular superstition. In His own day even the miraculous power of our Lord Himself [Elworthy's reference to Jesus] was considered by many of the Pharisees to be sorcery, or magic power, obtained by compact with Beelzebub,[38] whom all regarded as a personal being, and therefore they necessarily clothed him in actual form. [In the New Testament tale, some of the Pharisees regarded the miracles ascribed to Jesus as being performed through the arts of sorcery.]

From a serpent, which seems to be the oldest shape assigned to him, he developed into a dragon, that is a serpent with wings, having sometimes the head of a lion, sometimes of a man, and at others that of a crocodile.[39]

We must, in speaking of the devil, always remember the distinction between the dragon and the more classic griffin, whose body was that of a winged lion, with a head usually like an eagle, but with many modifications. Fig. 41 is the head of a griffin from the Forum of Trajan, in Rome, with a head of a lion, but horns of a goat, and hence of truly classic origin. In the Vatican Museum also, are several others to be seen with eagles' heads on lions' bodies, but with the fore feet like crocodiles' claws. Mr. Marindin says that the griffin is an attribute of Apollo, and (see Smith's *Dictionary of Antiquities*), "that some suppose the reason of the attribute, to be Apollo's supposed connexion with Hyperborean lands, where the Gryphes were supposed to dwell. . . . As to the Greek griffins, I suspect they are due to Assyrian influence. I believe one was found at Mycenae, and there is no doubt but Assyrian and Babylonian art influenced the Mycenaean, although the Mycenaean art was certainly a genuine water product." Schliemann says that the griffin came into Greece with Dionysos from India, and became the symbol of wisdom and enlightenment The griffin[40] is, however, very rare in ecclesiastical decoration, and we only certainly remember

Fig. 41. Forum of Trajan, Rome.

one example. Fig. 42 is from the doorway of the twelfth century cathedral at Scala, near Amalfi. One of these creatures guards each side of the entrance. The above sketches might perhaps be here somewhat out of place, were it not for the remarkable feature visible in both. Though the Scala figure is moulded with the fore legs of a wolf, the mane of a lion, and the head of an eagle, yet over all are the unmistakable horns; and so of the other, on the classic one from Rome, the horns are still more conspicuous. Both have likewise wings of a conventional kind. What horns may signify on these composite animals must be left for the reader to imagine and for experts to decide. Another feature

Fig. 42. Scala, Amalfi.

to be remarked is that the Roman head is somewhat canine, quite corresponding with the legs at Scala.[41]

It is evident, however, that the scriptural dragon must be considered as a development of the serpent, from the well-known passage,

"And he laid hold on the dragon, that old serpent, which is the devil." (Rev. xx. 2.) It is as a serpent-like dragon that he is shown fighting with St. Michael, and that myth is evidently identical with those of Horus, Perseus, and our own St. George, still perpetuated in this nineteenth century on the current coinage of our sovereigns and our crown pieces. As evidence that these stories are all one and the same myth, we may mention that in the Louvre is to be seen sculptured a high relief, though called *bas*, of "St. George and the Dragon," executed by Michel Colombe in 1508, but except in the size and shape of the dragon, and details of treatment, the incidents are precisely identical with a well-known picture contemporary with Colombe, in the Uffizi Gallery at Florence, by Pinturicchio, and there called "Perseus and Andromeda." Colombe represents St. George in plate armour piercing the dragon in the mouth with his tilting lance. The dragon is merely a monster crocodile, but the strange feature in this case is that in the background, upon a rock, is a kneeling female figure, dressed in the flowing robes of the six-teenth century, and with hands uplifted in the most stagey style of supplication. Truly here, Pegasus has lost his wings, while as a set off, Andromeda has found her clothes. So in these days the devil has lost his wings, but found a tail.

The confusion between the serpent and the dragon is of very ancient date, and probably found its way into Scripture after the return of the Jews from Babylonish captivity. According to ancient Chaldean belief regarding the fall, it was caused by Tiamat, the dragon of the sea, the female principle of evil, the original spirit of chaos, who, according to the Babylonians, older than the gods themselves, was self-existent, and eternal. It was the birth or separation of the deities out of Tiamat, that was the first step in the order and creation of the world. At length one of the gods had become the husband of the she-dragon (or serpent), and so kept alive the power of darkness. Then there was war, in which Bel, or Merodach (the sun god), volunteers to fight Tiamat. The descriptions of this fight, and subsequent triumph of the god representing the good principle over evil, of light over darkness, are said to be very fine. This Chaldean account has no correspondence with the narrative in Genesis, but is very suggestive of the contest between St. Michael and the dragon, as referred to above in Rev. xii.[42] Sometimes the devil is represented as a flying dragon.

A wood-cut by Albert Dürer, which the writer has seen only at Florence,[43] shows the dragon as a sort of hydra, with seven human heads, all of which bear distinct horns, and are all likewise crowned. These latter symbols are, we maintain, intended to show his might in conquest and his rank as king of the infernal hierarchy. Upon the pinnacle of Bow Church, Cheapside, the dragon appears as a flying crocodile. Thus it is through the serpent and the dragon forms, given him by the sacred writers, and so portrayed by mediaeval artists, that we get the ideas which have developed some of the peculiarities of the horned semi-human figure now commonly accepted. From these symbols of darkness grew his tail, which represents Apep of Egypt, the serpent of the Old Testament and of the Revelation, but not the Agathodemon of the classics.

In the earlier Egyptian mythology we find the prototype of Perseus and our St. George, in Horus slaying the dragon in both the forms of a serpent and of a crocodile. The *Book of the Dead*, p. 248 (Brit Mus. edition) has four different scenes. There does not appear in these to have been any Andromeda.

Many fanciful pictures, like Hone's, of St. Dunstan and the devil, give him a barbed tail like that of the fabulous dragon, a creature that was supposed to send fire out of its mouth with poisonous vapours; also called "the fiery flying serpent." (Isaiah xxx. 6.) This conventional dragon usually has a barbed tail. Moreover we often see one of the devil's feet, even when he has a human body, drawn with the three claws of the crocodile, as in a picture of the temptation by Lucas van Leyden, where the devil is represented as a monk with the dragon's foot peeping out beneath his gown, and the point of his cowl drawn out into a sort of tail like a serpent with its head at the end. This latter fancy is a mere reproduction of the same treatment, to be seen in the tail of the famous bronze Chimæra, in the Naples Museum. Leyden's picture, however, represents the devil without horns, unless they are supposed to be covered by the monk's cowl.

To find his horns and his hoofs in connection with any semblance of a human body we look in vain through the Scripture narrative, and hence the old artists, Dürer and L. van Leyden, were theologically correct; but the first glance at pagan mythology and classic art instantly unfolds the whole history.

We have remarked already that horns worn for honour or dignity were those of bulls or cows, while those of the ram and of the goat were used as symbols of fertility or the generative power. Moreover we read, that according to mediaeval belief all inhabitants of *ténébreux* wear horns as part of the infernal uniform, that they are liable to be forfeited by way of punishment or degradation (hence the Italian *scornare* previously discussed would have force even there). We are told that the phrase *porter les cornes* arose from our first mother Eve, who having obtained from the devil, the chieftain's horns he wore, as the price of her *complaisance*, presented them to her husband. [The tale that Elworthy references is not the biblical version. It is taken from the *Dictionary of the Infernal* by Collin De Plancy, published in 1818. Elworthy refers to Eve as "our first mother," which reflects his belief in the biblical tale of Adam and Eve as the first humans created by God.] Many stories of this kind might also be produced, but there was evidently the greatest confusion in the Middle Ages respecting the kind of horns with which to ornament the devil, for we find them of all kinds. Without going further back than the classic period, it will be sufficient to point out that the god Pan who in ancient Greece represented nature in its mere animal form was compounded of a man and a goat. He was the personification of lust and animal passions, but withal he was a merry, jovial being, full of rustic fun, of dance and song. The Pan-pipes, lasting till our own times, are still the recognised accompaniment of Punch and Judy shows, and remain the abiding witnesses to that side of the god's character. The same notion of his grim, mocking humour peeps out to-day in the gesture we have referred to and represented in Fig. 40, in spite of all the malignity, envy, and hatred which are usually associated with the spirit of evil.

We start then from the position that our modern conception of the personal appearance of the devil is the outcome of the Greco-Roman representations of the great god Pan, who, like all the other divinities, had his various attributes separately personified, especially as Liber and Priapus, the most licentious of all the Roman Pantheon; with these, however, our present discussion has no concern. We shall therefore attempt no more here than to show the various stages of his growth into the creature now commonly accepted.

Fig. 43 is from a Roman bronze lamp, and represents Pan standing upon the back of a tortoise. There is nothing special about this; he is shown as always, unclothed, with goat's legs and hoofs, and in this case the horns are rather more like those of a ram than a goat;

Fig. 43. Fortunio Liceto.

but although we know that the goat, and not the ram, was Pan's special relative, yet we are told that rams and cows were sacrificed to him as the god of flocks and herds. The ancient artists, too, like their mediaeval and modern successors, were not always realistically true to nature, and, moreover, were sometimes guilty of mistakes in their treatment. We have seen pictures by so-called "old masters" of the doctors in the temple disputing with our Lord, and wearing very modern-looking, steel-framed spectacles; and we have heard of Abel being shot with a pistol. Further, it will be noticed that the lamp (Fig. 44), which the vine leaves prove to represent Bacchus, has very distinct goat's horns, and we are told that Bacchus, or Dionysos, also a lascivi-

Fig. 44. Fortunio Liceto.

ous god, is but another aspect of Pan. [**This idea bears no merit as Dionysus is a complex deity with aspects that are much higher in Nature than Pan. Any in-depth study of mythology will readily demonstrate that these are two distinct deities, neither one being an aspect of the other.**] There are also several varieties of goats now, as there must have been always, and some have horns much more curled than others. The attitude of Pan depicted upon the tortoise by no means gives the idea of a merry being, but Fig. 45, which shows the head in a well-known group of Pan and Bacchus in the Villa Ludovisi, gives a much better notion of the half human, half bestial face, the true foundation on which has grown up the modern, vulgar, merry devil.

Here, too, the horns are not very goat-like, but a good deal conventionalised, evidently to suit the exigencies of marble sculpture; but the fact with which we are most concerned remains, they are a distinct feature. The whole figure in this statue corresponds admirably with the countenance, and being placed in a very public spot, may well have represented, not only the then prevalent ideal, but have so impressed itself upon the minds of the people as to become a tradition lasting down even to our own times. Moreover, in considering this tradition we must not forget that the same Roman people had before them

Fig. 45. Rome.

other horned heads on many important statues. For instance, in the Vatican Museum is a bust (No. 232) called "Giove in forma di Bue," which is simply the head of an ox on human shoulders. Again, in the Villa Albani is a group representing Theseus slaying the Minotaur, a very remarkable statue, inasmuch as it represents the monster with the body of a man and the head of a bull. Further, the Romans were still more familiar with representations of the Minotaur in the shape of a bull with a human head, well-horned, as on the Sicilian coins. (Figs. 9, 10, p. 18.)

This latter, the usual form of the Minotaur, was probably the more popular idea, and is more in accordance with Greek models received by the Greeks from Egypt, who in their turn, doubtless represented and modified those of the earlier Chaldeans, shown in the man-faced bulls in the British Museum. Being so accustomed to the various forms of the Minotaur, on which the horns were never omitted, whether the head were human or bovine, we may easily account for the confusion as to Pan in the popular mind, through which tradition had to percolate. In fact, "All the gods were one,"[44] sang Orpheus, and we know that Bacchus (called Bicorniger) had horns, Jupiter had horns, Pan had horns; therefore we cannot wonder if we find those of the bull, the ram, the goat used indifferently, and often wrongly. When we find our modern devil then with the horns of any one of those animals, our chain of sequence is not broken, for they have been conventional symbols even from Roman times. We know, however, that Pan, the prototype, should properly have goat's horns, as shown on the typical mask of Pan (Fig. 46) placed

Fig. 46. Museo Campidoglio, Rome.

above the famous Amazon sarcophagus in the Capitoline Museum at Rome.

Another example (Fig. 47) from a group in the Naples Museum is almost identical in subject with that from which Fig. 45 was taken. Here the body is the same half man, half goat, and the countenance though different, has an equally bestial expression, and represents as clearly in the original as a face can, all the low animal passions on which we have been dwelling, as well as the malignity of the more intellectual being we connect with the name of Satan [For modern Pagans, animals are not viewed as lowly in nature compared to humans. Instead they are beings in tune with the

HORNS OF HONOR

natural order of things, who can act as guides and messengers. They can also appear as omens and signs.]

That even in the classic age a more human face was often given to fauns and satyrs (the latter name only signifies older fauns, the offspring of such beings as in later days were called incubi and succubae) is proved not only by such exquisite works of art as the fauns of Praxiteles and the dancing faun at Florence, but by other works of ancient sculptors. Some of these latter clearly show a transition between the true Pan-like countenance and the beauty of those last referred to, even though the beautiful fauns were of much earlier date.

Fig. 47. Lateran Museum. Rome.

Fig. 48 (page 100) represents the heads of two Hermae now in the museum of St. John Lateran. In the originals the expression of both is wonderful. The horns are merely symbols retained to express the character of the being represented, and are even shown to be artificial and no growth, by being fastened to a fillet passing round the head. The relationship to Pan is shown by the pointed ears and goat-like beard, but there all resemblance ceases. Along with features showing marked power and intellect, we see an expression which is well understood, but which we can only describe as devilish. Here are faces uniting the Satan of Milton, of Faust, or Lucio in Miss Corelli's book, with the mere animal, lustful Pan. As represented by these modern authors the devil is more beautiful in feature, yet none could be more fascinating than these faces in the originals, or more clearly show the grandeur of ancient sculpture in portraying character. All who are interested in this subject are strongly recommended, if opportunity should arise, to examine the statues themselves, whence these two heads are but rudely sketched. The heads are about life size.

Leaping over many centuries, during which the Gnostic ideas had their full sway, and brought art down to a very low estate, we next come to a strange period—that of the Knights Templar of the twelfth and thirteenth centuries. We do not meddle with the accusations, trials, or suppression of that body, beyond noticing the fact that many of the crimes with which they were charged, were

Fig. 48.

before their time laid as accusations against the early Christians, and since their time have been both revived and kept alive to this day against the Jews. Some of the most atrocious criminal charges of which many Templars were pronounced guilty, and for which they were put to death, are to this day in some countries preferred against the Jews, and no doubt implicitly believed; but it is to the credit of modern justice, that even where the intensest *judenhetze* prevails, there has never been an approach to a legal conviction. Without entering, however, into the controversy, we give in Fig. 49 two aspects of Baphomet, whom the Templars were accused of worshipping, and who is represented by their accusers to be the devil. They are taken from a well-known controversial work—Von Hammer-Purgstall's *Baphometum Revelatum*. There is no evidence that the Templars either intended these, and other figures they have left behind, to represent the devil, or that they actually worshipped them, any more than other figures in the most orthodox of Christian Churches are worshipped to-day; but the popular and the clerical imagination in the thirteenth century believed them to be intended for the devil, and thus we get some further though slight evidence of what the people of those days thought he was like. It is very probable that the horns on one of the figures suggested the devil. The sun, moon, and cross upon the other should have satisfied their accusers.

Fig. 49.

One feature in these figures is remarkable, and might have instigated these charges against the Templars. It will be seen that both figures are hermaphrodite, and this may have appealed to those who, as we have seen, believed that the evil one could assume human form in either sex at his will. We know from statues and paintings that the belief in androgynous human beings was prevalent among the Romans. The most famous is perhaps the statue in the Villa Borghese, but there is another in the Naples Museum, and there are also Pompeian frescoes of the same kind. We can easily account for the Templars' ideal, seeing that they received so much of their peculiar cult through the Gnostics, whose fancies in the direction of combination between human beings and all kinds of creatures, evidently bore much fruit in the pictorial representation of demons in the Middle Ages.[45]

Only one of these Baphomets is horned upon his head, but it will be noticed that the other in female attire has the horned crescent upon the arm and also the sun upon the breast, and it is worth noting once more, *en passant*, that upon the breasts of both the well-horned North American Indian chiefs, Figs. 7, 8, we also find the sun very plainly painted. So far as the sun and moon upon the arm and breast of Baphomet are concerned, the Templars could be no more accused of idolatry than the Dean and Chapter of Wells, whose seal of a later date we show in Fig. 88. Except in the horns, there is little in the Templars' so-called idol to suggest any kinship to the classic Pan; yet it is the horns of our modern devil that we are endeavouring to account for, and nearly every example we come across in every land from the early Middle Ages gives him horns upon his head.

The monkish ideas of the time of the Templars seem rather to invest him with St. Peter's description in 1 Peter v. 8, "as a roaring lion," but still the horns are not forgotten, though the features are often so much conventionalised that they suit no beast in particular.

To illustrate this notion we give Figs. 50, 51, the heads of two of the famous devils of Notre Dame de Paris, probably not much later than Baphomet. The bodies are only modelled as far as the waist, but in each case they are, except the head, human in form, and as usual, nude. The artist who designed them seemed rather to desire to make them hideous and savage, than to represent any known animal, though the goat's beard is shown in one. Perhaps these heads were his idea of what a dragon's head was like.

Figs. 50, 51. Notre Dame.

Fig. 52 (on page 104) is of a much higher type, and is the work of a famous artist, John of Bologna, the sculptor of the well-known Mercury now in the Bargello at Florence, a statue, perhaps, more copied than any other work of the Italian renaissance.

The little bronze figure here sketched has a history which we have recorded elsewhere. It was, however, designed avowedly, and placed where it was, upon the outer angle of a palace, as a devil to keep off the devil, and has been known for centuries as "il diavolino." This figure, though a good deal conventionalised, is manifestly Pan with the head of "a roaring lion." His horns are, however, much curtailed—still there they are—the artist's notions of propriety caused him to keep them small and inconspicuous. In this

Fig. 52. Florence.

thoroughly composite figure we cannot fail to see a representation of both the scriptural and the classical conceptions—the lion's head and mane of that "old serpent the dragon," and the horns and body of the goat-man Pan. His tail is wanting, but so are those of the figures on Notre Dame, and we may well conclude that the head is the feature which is meant to signify and not the tail. Indeed his tail seems to have grown upon the devil quite in modern times.

The Florentine diavolino is really a beautiful little work of art, but of the thousands of tourists who visit Florence few have ever heard of it, and far fewer still have ever seen it, but we urge all future visitors who may read these lines to examine it, in order to be able to judge what in the Middle Ages was the popular idea of the devil's form and likeness. The original is now removed to the Bargello, while a copy is installed in its place.

Another example we take from Florence, are approximately of the same age. Fig. 53 is from a large fresco in the Chapter House,

now called the Capella degli Spagnuoli, in the Church of Santa
Maria Novella, painted in 1332. It is said to be by Simone Memmi
of Sienna, according to Vasari, but other good
authorities attribute the picture to the school
of Giotto, of whom there are some undoubted
works close by; but seeing that Memmi was a
pupil of Giotto, the objection is rather hypercrit-
ical. There is, however, some confusion on this
point among the authorities.

Fig. 53.

The face in this example seems to represent extreme and violent
malignity, coupled with a good deal of intellectual power. The body
too, is human, though furnished with bat-like dragon's wings. The
horns, however, are very remarkable, and different to any we remember; and they add much to the fierceness of the head.

In the well-known fresco in the Vatican called the "Dispute
of the Sacrament" Raphael has portrayed Satan with a handsome,
intellectual face, but a diabolical expression; on his head, however,
are the inevitable horns—large, goatlike, and conspicuous.

In the British Museum is a print of a Last Judgment by Fra
Angelico, in which the devil is represented with a human body,
and bat-like wings, but the head is a gaping, roaring bull, with high
branching horns.

Another print, by Marco Antonio, represents the devil with a
repulsive human countenance, high horns rising from a bald head,
bat's wings, and eagle's legs.

Fig. 54 is from a picture by Liberale da Verona, also in the Uffizi,
c. 1530. The devil is represented as floating in the air, an early example
of the fashion then first appearing of painting heads with the wings

only of a dragon. The painting of winged heads without bodies ran riot, both in stone and on canvas, in the seventeenth and eighteenth centuries, and has not yet disappeared from some of our country churches, though the heads now are made as infantile and as beautiful as they began in ugliness—a development that cannot fail to call to

Fig. 54.

mind the story of the Gorgon, which being at first the type of fearsome hideousness, grew at last into the Strozzi Medusa, and that on the Tassa Farnese, considered to be the very ideals of female beauty; so that the face which once had fascinated and turned men to stone by its fearfulness, came to be considered at last to work the same charm by its loveliness. Thus the devil has become a cherub. The demon shown in the latter sketch gives the idea of low cunning and ribald mockery, while the mouth denotes gross animal passions, mixed with intense malignity. The horns are not so prominent, but they are a distinct feature of the head, and although they are a good deal conventionalised by the fancy of the master, yet nevertheless they are present, and are, indeed, veritable horns.

It would be easy to multiply examples, and to produce them from every decade down to the present day, but enough has been shown to prove the general accordance in European Art from the time of the Greek Pan down to the very end of the nineteenth century. One feature of the devil's appearance—his horns—has been so thoroughly recognised as belonging to him, that in what shape soever he is represented, it is almost never omitted. In the Far East it is the same. The most fearful faces are given to all representations of Chinese and Japanese devils, retaining, nevertheless, a general human form; though in that respect they are by no means like the heads from Notre Dame and Florence (Figs. 50, 51, 52); yet in every case we have seen, the horns are as conspicuous as ever. In the Naples Museum is a little black Indian figure in terra cotta; human all but the face; the body is nude and ill-shaped, with exaggerated belly; the face is beaked like an eagle, with no trace of humanity, but above all are the inevitable, conspicuous, branching horns. While the Indian keeps to the Aryan type, the Mongolian idea however seems wholly apart from the Greek Pan. The Chinese figures are clothed more or less in Eastern fashion, and seem but very distantly related, if at all, to Indian conceptions of destructive and malignant beings, but the horns are never omitted.

We give one more example, not only because it represents the usual and common form of Japanese devil, but simply because the horns are so much like the European conventional type, that they prove the almost universality of the belief, or rather the idea, we have been seeking to illustrate.

Fig. 55 is from a mask[46] sketched at Mr. Bowes's Japanese Museum, Liverpool, evidently intended to represent a face of the utmost ferocity and malignity.

Of course it is but a mask, yet it is quite as valuable for our purpose as the representation of the living head. We started with a mask of Pan, which nearly two millenniums before expressed the Roman idea of the nature-god—partly joyous, partly terrible, and we have seen how that same idea has shaped itself in passing through a long succession of minds in various ages and

Fig. 55.

among many nations. We have seen how all the bright side, except the simplicity or gullibility, has been gradually eliminated, until we have in the Far East, as in the Far West, the conception of a being altogether bestial, ferocious, and base. Even where the hideous and the terrible are modified by a laugh, that very laugh has degenerated, and so become the expression of something still more malignant, the raging, maleficent grin of fiendish mockery, or, on the other hand, the merely stupid, vulgar comicality of *Punch*.

Fig. 56.

Perhaps the very latest serious home representation still existing of modern notions of the devil, which we may compare with its Japanese contemporary, is shown in Fig. 56. This is called the *Dorset Ooser*, and the sketch is taken from a photograph in *Somerset and Dorset Notes and Queries*, vol. ii. (1891), p. 289. It is a wooden mask of large size with features grotesquely human, long flowing locks of hair on either side of the head, a beard, and a pair of bullock's horns projecting right and left of the forehead. It is cut from a solid block of wood; the lower jaw is movable by the wearer. The Ooser, here represented, belongs to Mr. Cave, of Holt Farm, Melbury Osmond Dorset, "in whose family it has been preserved time out of mind." It is not, however, probable that it is older than the last century, though it may be the relic of a very ancient custom and the latest survivor of a long line of similar masks, which time and decay have eaten up. It was probably worn at the village revel, and may even have been used at some of the miracle plays, that certainly lasted down to Elizabethan times, after the Reformation had been completely established. Hobby horses were very common, and well within the present century, at the feast of St. Michael, a sort of revel or fair was kept up at Minehead, in which a hideous figure called a hobby horse used to frighten girls and children, holding great pincers and "acting the devil." The writer's mother once witnessed this performance in her youth, and often described it. There does not appear to have been any pretence of a horse, though called a hobby horse, but simply a man with a mask and made up as a devil. The pincers seem to have impressed her, but she used not to speak of horns, and in those days their importance had not become so apparent to the writer as to lead to particular questions, but we doubt not their having been present nevertheless. There are plenty of entries in old churchwardens' accounts of payments made to "mynstrellis," and for the hobby horse. Many inquiries have been made of the oldest inhabitants, but no detailed account of the performance can be got at Minehead, although several say they "mind it" or have "a-yeard tell o' it." What has so soon passed out of mind at Minehead may also have done the like at Melbury, but it is none the less interesting to possess this probable head of the hobby horse. The name it bears in Dorset is not so easy to explain. The late Rev. W. Barnes, who never hesitated, says: "Ooser, oose or wuse—a mask as with grim jaws, put on with a cow's skin to frighten folk. 'Wurse,' in Layamon's *Brut*, is the name of the arch-fiend."

The summary infallible method is not however always to be accepted, and even if the above have any germ of probability, the cart is put before the horse. We find no sort of evidence that the mask was ever called a *wuse*, and no reference being vouchsafed we cannot verify the *wurse*.

If the show itself be a relic of monkish plays, a realistic method of terrifying people by the sight of monsters and "fiery trials," we may well look to the same source for some relics of the words by which the protagonist in them was named and described. In our western dialect these words are much longer lived than the stage properties of the miracle plays, and in our common word *soce* we still retain the *socius* or *socii* of the monastery, just as *socius* remains in full force to-day among the "notions" of the "Winchester Gentlemen." So we venture to suggest that *osor* was perhaps the favourite name for the person to whom it was applied in the Morris Dances and Mysteries. It is true that no contemporary authority is available, but the same objection applies to *soce*[47] and to many another vernacular word, which the people remember and hand down with their own pronunciation and their own special meaning attached to them. When we see as we do, modern authors using words because "they sound quaint" without knowing or taking the pains to find out what they really mean, we cannot wonder if the "clerks" of unlearned times did likewise, and often set down words of which they did not know the meaning, while they omitted many of the people's words, just as they do now, as too common for literature.

There was an old French word *oseur*, but we are not aware of its having been used as a name for the devil. The word *osor*, though not to be found in the better-known mediaeval Latin writers, is however a recognised word in Plautus, while in searching for something else, we found in Gori the expression "Osor et hostis acerrimus" used as a name for Diabolus Christiani. The above are of course mere suggestions, and by no means offered as a philological solution of a very difficult question.

Examining this *ooser*, one is struck by the persistency of certain well-discussed features. The horns truly are very bovine, still they are a very conspicuous element in the whole, and obviously intended to be so. We have, however, already discussed this question sufficiently, but it should be noted that, while the beard and side locks have no sort of connection with the ox or cow, yet they do very plainly keep alive and bring us back to the distinctive traits of the goat. The eyes and nose are simply frightful without special meaning; but the grinning, opening and shutting jaws reproduce that voracious, malignant mockery which we have seen to be the conspicuous attribute of the devil from the Middle Ages onwards to our own day, whether in England or Japan.

Modern travellers tell us that the mystery plays in which the devil performs a principal part, are still kept up and commonly practised in Mexico. A number of photographs of the *dramatis personarum* have been shown to the writer by Mr. William Corner, in which the devil bears the usual horns. These things are, of course, the result of Spanish intercourse. The Folklore Society have recently deposited at Cambridge a large number of the objects connected with these plays, the gift of Professor Starr, of Chicago.

Very much more might be said upon this large subject of the devil, but we have felt it to be beyond the limits of our present task to do more than roughly sketch the facts, with such a selection of illustrations as may show what is the present popular conception of the devil's bodily appearance and how it has grown up. The general history of the devil we studiously avoid, and least of all do we desire to enter into the modern controversy of his personal existence. Those who desire to pursue that branch of the subject, or to verify the statements we have made, will find in the books we have quoted sufficient suggestions of the enormous bibliography existing, which has been the source from which we have drawn our facts. Moreover, to the serious student the abundant further references he will find in the more scholarly of the books, form such a mass of material as will enable him to so probe the question to the bottom, as fully to occupy the full term of his natural life.

Long since this was written has appeared the part of the *Historical English Dictionary*, containing several pages on the word *horn*. A study of these pages by Dr. Murray will prove them to be a veritable epitome of all that can be said upon the subject, and will provide abundant quotations in illustration of most of the facts we have adduced. Nevertheless it is hoped the foregoing facts may not thereby be deprived of their interest.

CHAPTER III.

The Hand

Tʜᴇ ᴘʀᴇsᴇɴᴛ ᴡʀɪᴛᴇʀ ʜᴀs already dealt at some length with this member, well named by Aristotle "the tool of tools." Hitherto he has, however, but approached the fringe of the subject, and produced the merest sample of the facts concerning it.

To touch and to handle, though undoubtedly its most important functions, are, even amongst us matter-of-fact English people, but a small part of the uses for which our hands come into practice.

Putting aside all notice of palmistry and mesmerism into which the hand so largely enters, and leaving those departments to the experts who make a special business of such quasi-sciences, there is an abundant field for observation even without going beyond our own four seas; whilst among more emotional people than ourselves the hands play a part which, though often referred to, has in only one work with which we are acquainted been treated in anything approaching a systematic manner.[48] Much use has been made of this book, but chiefly in connection with that branch of manual gesture so common among the Italians, which expresses their belief in, and their actions to ward off, the effects of *jettatura* or *malocchio*.[49]

Elsewhere, we have given an elaborate system of manual numeration, said by the Abate Requeno to have been obtained by the Romans from the Greeks, by which any number, up to hundreds of thousands, could be signalled by the hands alone.

Another system, similar in kind but very different in the manual signs, is given, also with full illustrations, by Zornius, *Bibliotheca Antiquaria*, vol. ii. p. 793.

Among ourselves even, gesticulation, though restrained as a rule, and moderate by comparison, is of course common enough, whether we study the actions of the real orator, the cushion-thumping preacher, or the hand-washing-with-impalpable-water-and-invisible-soap of the obsequious shopman. The devotional attitude of the hands is just as well understood by us English of to-day as it was by the Minutoli of Naples in the thirteenth century, shown in Fig. 23, thus proving that six hundred years of time and over a thousand miles of space, have had no effect in even modifying what seems to be, by the common consent of mankind, the most

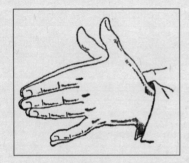

Fig. 57.

appropriate manual gesture with which to accompany his devotions.

It is, moreover, curious as well as instructive to note that the same placing of the hands together, as in Fig. 57, is in Neapolitan gesture language the sign for the expression *stupidity*.[150] Assuming that the mere helpless laying of the hands flatly together, in fact placing the hands in a position both of absolute inoffensiveness and defencelessness, seems always to have been a symbol of humble submission, of weak inferiority; we can then readily perceive how "the lifting up" of the hands,[50] in that same position shown in the frontispiece (p. ii), has, so far as we know, always been the one appropriate for Christians, to mark the approach of a mere man in adoration, to the presence of his Maker; or to offer up his supplications to Almighty God. A study of the two gestures shown and referred to above makes evident the importance of the "lifting up" of the hands, for in the Neapolitan gesture of *stupidity* they are distinctly held downwards or towards the person addressed, thus conveying the imputation away from the gesticulator to the addressee; while by lifting them up a supplicatory attitude is assumed, which implies that the ignorance, weakness, and stupidity are the property of him who thus poses his hands in prayer or devotion. Careful examination will assure the most cursory observer that all our own well-known manual gestures are not simple conventionalities, the outcome of accident, but that each has some distinct meaning, and is the outward expression of some inward feeling. The special one we have been considering seems to be common to at least all Christian people, and the writer believes it can be shown not only in early Greek sculpture, but in that of the much earlier Egypt and Chaldaea. In Neapolitan gesture, as is well known, the same pose of the fingers has all the difference in the world in meaning, when held in different positions.

We find that manual gestures appropriate to different devotions, as well as to different divinities, enter so largely into the worship of Oriental people, as to have acquired separate technical names. The *mudrâ*, of the Hindoo, for which we have no equivalent word in English, is not only the name for the elaborate hand and finger signs with which he accompanies his *sandhyâ* or morning prayer, and without which he believes it to be ineffectual, but it is also the name for the expressive manual positions of the gods themselves. This may be seen on various Indian carvings, such as those upon the great rock sculptures of Bamian. Moor's *Hindoo Pantheon* and Calmet's *Dictionary of the Bible* supply very many examples of these, from which we have taken the annexed illustrations. It will be noted that every one of these gestures of ancient Assyrian or modern Indian gods have their exact counterparts in either Neapolitan or sacerdotal

Fig. 58. Brahma Vishnu (Moor 5).

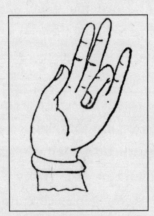

Fig. 59. Parvati (Moor 102).

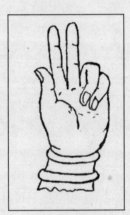

Fig. 60. Vishnu (Moor 101).

Fig. 61 Dagon (Calmet). Brahma (Moor, 32).

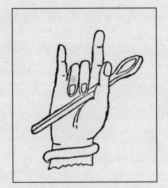

Fig. 62. Brahma (Moor, 3).

Fig. 63. Dagon (Calmet). Lakshmi (Moor, 8).

gestures of to-day. The Buddhists of China and Japan, no less than the Hindoos, hold the position of the hands and fingers to be of the utmost importance. They recognise the attributes of Amitâbha, the Buddhist Jehovah, by nine distinct signs or finger gestures, which, though differing in many details, yet forcibly recall the system of manual numeration given as ancient Greek by the Abate Requeno.

One Japanese sect worship their Buddha by simply making before him as a mystic rite, certain prescribed gestures, a sort of manual speech, but without any form of words, which they call *shin-mitsu*. No doubt in our superiority we may be inclined to treat this performance with some contempt, but we should not forget that this is only because we do not know by what private prayers it is accompanied; and before condemning others for acts of mere ritual, practised according to their light, we should remember that a Japanese would, on his part, just as little understand our doings in the manual actions so definitely prescribed in the Christian order for consecration, *i.e.* the laying on of hands, practised by all Christian people, whether Roman, Greek, Lutheran, Anglican, or Nonconformist, and whether or not prescribed in a rubric. Far less would he comprehend the manual gestures so distinctly ordered in baptism and other Christian rites.

Much instruction may be gathered from a study of comparative religious gesture, and it is something more than a remarkable coincidence when we find that the identical gesture shown in Fig. 64, that of extending the three fingers of the right hand while joining the thumb and forefinger, is not only that of Brahma and of the Hindoo god Vishnu, as shown

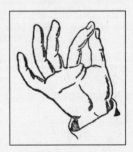

Fig. 64. Jorio, Pl. 20.

by Moor, Fig. 58, but it is that of a Roman priest when he blesses his flock, either during the mass or when he passes in procession amongst them. In making the sign of the cross during the mass, the celebrant is ordered to turn the little finger of the right hand, keeping the right hand straight with the fingers extended and joined together at the thumb. This position of his hand is minutely prescribed in the rubric.

In the British Museum may be seen a large image of the Chinese goddess *Kwan-yin*, having four arms on each side. One pair has hands posed horizontally, as in the last illustration, with finger and thumb touching.[51]

A pair of hands on this same goddess, but in a smaller figure, are raised up above the rest, in the same attitude as Dagon, Lakshmi, Parvati, and as the Dextera Dei from the clouds in Figs. 64, 66. This is the position now used in final benediction in the Greek Church. Another pair of hands on this same figure are in the attitude so well known as the *mano cornuta*—that of St. Luke, and of Brahma (Figs. 61, 62). The Japanese god *Avalokiteswara* has no less than twenty-four hands on a regular sheaf of arms on either side. Of these, there are three pairs posed in *mano cornuta*, *i.e.*, fore and little fingers extended, while all the rest are evidently in carefully designed attitudes. Another pair are in one of the positions of Vishnu and Brahma, shown on Fig. 58, which is likewise the gesture of a Moslem when he recites his creed; it is, as stated above, the sign of justice, perfection, and of menace in the Neapolitan gesture language, according to Jorio, when held horizontally, and of love when uplifted. Lastly a hand in this attitude is one of the common amulets against *jettatura*, to be purchased of Neapolitan shopkeepers in coral, silver, or mother-of-pearl, and it may be often seen upon the backs of cab-horses in the streets. Doubtless further investigation would find this special sign in use for many other purposes.

To convince the reader how important is manual gesture in Christian, as well as in Japanese ritual, he will find that the way in which the priest's hand is to be used is carefully prescribed in the rubrics pertaining to Christian baptism.

In the *Rituale Romanum*, we read: "Deinde intigit pollicem in sacro chrismate, et ungit infantem in summitate capitis in modum crucis, dicens Deus Omnipotens, etc. . . . Postea pollice faciat signum crucis in fronte et in pectore infantis." The same direction is repeated in the rubrics for Extreme Unction, Confirmation, Ordination of Priests, Coronation, and Consecration of an Altar. So again it is customary in Anglican baptism to christen with the thumb, doubtless traditional from pre-Reformation usage, and easily to be traced back to so-called paganism. The thumb extended as a manual gesture is not confined to Christian ritual, for under the Jewish dispensation we find that in the order for the consecration of priests, set out in Holy Writ, the thumb of the right hand, as well as the great toe of the right foot,[52] are specially mentioned there several times, and, moreover, they are the only parts of his body to which the consecrating blood is ordered to be applied, proving the high ceremonial importance in which the thumb was held—particularly that of the right hand.

Hence also we perceive why the ceremony of restoring a healed leper to life and liberty was completed by the application of the oil by the priest to his right thumb and the great toe of the right foot.

Moslems, too, many of whose rites are Jewish, hold the thumb as of high importance. We read that Turks at the rite of circumcision, which takes place at eight years (and not at eight days according to Jewish law), are compelled to recite, "There is but one God, and Mahommed is His messenger," with thumb erect. Again, before the oration in the mosque, they announce the names of the faithful who are in *articulo mortis* with the thumb upraised; and the priests in funeral processions chant with the thumb raised in the same way. We are told by the Abbé Huc that in Thibet the mendicant Lama goes about asking alms with the hand clenched but with the thumb pointing upwards.[53] We know, too, that in ancient Rome it was usual at the gladiatorial shows for the audience, even the women, to signify by raising or depressing the thumb whether the defeated gladiator should be spared or dispatched.

Our forefathers the Belgae, we are told, would place no faith in the signature of the Danish king until he had impressed his thumb upon the wax, thus adding his seal thereto. Some of us can testify that this mode of sealing is by no means even yet extinct.

Whether we look at its position in the celebration of the mass, when the ordinary *pax vobiscum* is pronounced, as before explained, or in the higher sacerdotal act of ceremonial benediction, to which we shall refer later; or whether we regard its use as conveying power and authority such as is distinctly implied by the "laying on of hands" by bishops and others, we cannot but admit that a very important function is accorded to the hand, in various parts of religious ritual, by all Christians, Hebrews, and by many others, some of whom we are accustomed to speak of as infidel or idolatrous. In this aspect it is quite easy to trace the same underlying idea of the importance of manual gesture pictorially shown in the practices of the ancient Egyptians, and continued from the days of Israel in Egypt down to comparatively recent times amongst ourselves.

We see by Fig. 65 how in sculpture in the tombs at Tel-el-Amarna every ray of the life-giving sun is made to terminate in a hand, and how one of these hands is presenting the ankh, or symbol of life, to the lips of the royal worshipper. An examination of this and the following illustrations will be sufficient evidence to prove the continuance of the same idea down to the Christian period of the Middle Ages.

Fig. 65. At Tel-el-Amarna.

On Fig. 66, from an early Bible, the rays are descending from the tips of the fingers, of a hand reaching down from above, upon the head of a king (Charles the Bald), and in Figs. 67, 68 (page 122), the rays are also descending through the hand, directly from the hand of the Almighty.

In one of these (Fig. 66) the hand is open, as in the Tel-el-Amarna sculpture; in another (Fig. 67) it is in the position used by the early Church in the act of solemn benediction, and still retained by the Greek

Fig. 66.

Fig. 67 (top).
Fig. 68 (right).

Church as the gesture appropriate to that act. This latter illustration is from a MS. of the tenth century, and the manual sign, so carefully drawn, must be looked at in connection with the life-giving rays proceeding from it, and the whole undoubtedly signifies that both life and blessing are being poured down by one and the same act.

In the other example, in Fig. 68, which is a century later, we find the same idea, with the important difference that no special gesture is implied by the hand, which here represents simply the power of the Almighty; while the rays passing from the hand are in the form of a sheaf of spears.[54]

Of a much earlier period than these are the mosaics in the Church of San Vitale, at Ravenna, dating not later than the sixth century. Fig. 69 on page 123 is from a sketch made of one of them. Here Moses is bidden to take off his shoes, etc. The command is conveyed by the *dextera Dei* from the clouds, posed precisely in the way we have been discussing.

Regarding the tenth century illumination, Fig. 67, we may observe that it is very unusual to find this gesture depicted in a Latin Church document so long after the schism of the churches in the eighth century.

In all these cases the idea is precisely the same: in Egypt the rays pass from the sun's disc into and thence from the hand, while in Christian art they appear to come from the hand alone. The source of the power to be conveyed is from above, *i.e.*, from the supreme deity, plainly denoted by the visible sun of the Egyptian, and by the unseen Almighty of the Christian, whose hand only is exhibited.

Fig. 69.

The open hand, coming down from above, is also found without any visible rays, as in Fig. 70, from a Saxon MS. "indicative of the Divine favour"; Fig. 71 is from an Exulter of the eleventh century, showing a different pose. Another hand from the clouds in the position in the last example is over a crucifix outside the south door of Romsey Abbey Church—both (Figs. 70, 71) are from Twining's *Symbols*, etc., Plate II., p. 6.

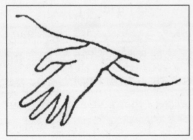

Fig. 70.

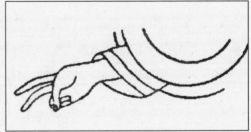

Fig. 71.

The power of the human hand itself is an article of very ancient belief, and remains almost unaltered to this day. When Naaman was wroth with Elisha, it was because he did not "strike" his hand over the place—not to touch, but to make those manual passes with the hand which to this day are believed to be effectual. To "bless vore," as it is called in the *Exmoor Scolding*, and as practised still, is to do precisely what Naaman expected to see done to his leprous spot. In this nineteenth century, in Somerset, the word used for the application of any ointment or liniment is the Biblical "to strike"; moreover, ointment or other medicament should always be applied by the *digitus medicus*. The common remedy for that well-known inflammatory swelling of the eyelid, called a "stye," is to "strike" it three times with a wedding-ring, held between the thumb and third finger.

Elsewhere we have referred to the present belief in Somerset that the hand of a corpse is effectual to cure a goitre, if caused to "strike" three times over it. Especially is this held if the hand be that of a man that has been hung. We refer to this again later.

The "lifting up" of the hand to which allusion has been made, applied rather to the attitude of raising than to the special pose of the hand itself, but it applied to all kinds of finger positions. The hands in the frontispiece, for example, are distinctly lifted up. The gesture referred to by the psalmist in Psalm cxxxiv, 2, cxli, 2 is the open hand with the palm outwards. This seems to have been, and to be still, the attitude of adoration, while that depicted on the Minutoli, Fig. 24, is that peculiar to prayer. Often both hands together were uplifted,[55] but when one only was so uplifted, it is always the "right hand of power" that is depicted. It will be seen that it is the right hand which is held up by all the actors (Fig. 65), in adoration of the sun while receiving the gift of life from the right-handed ray. In further demonstration of this fact, we call attention to one of two similar primitive statuettes from Tetini, Sardinia (Fig. 72); not only does it show the uplifting of the right hand, but it is a good example of the fact already noted elsewhere, that the pose of the hand in ancient art was always carefully studied in every representation, whether in painting or sculpture, and never to be overlooked in judging of the meaning, for example, of a scene on a painted vase, or the personality or *motif* of any statue. The exaggeration in the hand marks the significance of the gesture. All this applies with equal force to the gestures of Hindoo, Chinese, and Japanese deities, as depicted by Calmet and Moor (*ante*), and may be studied on many examples to be seen in the British Museum. The attitude of respect among the ancient Egyptians was just as it is to-day

Fig. 72.

throughout the East, to put the right hand upon the breast, but the usual mode of standing in the presence of a superior was with the hand passed across the breast to the opposite shoulder.

The uplifted, open hand was probably one of the signs or gestures brought by Israel out of Egypt, and the *Jadh* still holds among the chosen people a very prominent place. Not only does the modern Jew raise his open right hand, when in a court of justice he covers his head to take a solemn oath upon the sacred law, but in Jerusalem especially he paints the open hand in bright vermilion, or carves it over his door. The Moslem does the same; indeed, an open hand may be seen over the doors of both Jews and Mohammedans alike in Tunis, also over the great gate of the Alhambra. It has been suggested that this hand denoted Justice, over the Puerto del Perdon, but tradition points to its being the hand of victory, described below, for the legend was that the Alhambra could not be taken till the hand above grasped the key beneath. The figure under the arch is, of course, a Spanish insertion. Moreover, we show later that *la main de la justice* was posed in a different manner. The reverence paid to the open hand on the column on St. Sophia at Constantinople has been already referred to elsewhere. We are told also that the Vice-President of America, on taking office, takes the oath "with uplifted hand."[56] The same open hand is painted on the robe of the North American chief Mahtawopah. (Fig. 7.)

The open hand, when uplifted, was the sign of victory. It was this same hand—an open hand—that Saul set up at Carmel (I Samuel xv. 12), where he is said to have "set him up a place" in token of his victory over Agag and the Amalekites. The translation "a place," as given in the A.V., can have no meaning at all; but the Hebrew writer and also the Greek translator knew well that *hand* alone was the important word.[57]

The open hand set up as a trophy or token of triumph was the usual symbol of the Phoenicians. It appears on many of their stelae or monumental tablets, with which Saul and the Israelites must have been quite familiar. The spot referred to in the above text was near to Tyre, where doubtless this uplifted hand was the common sign.

They may therefore with confidence be maintained to be precisely what Saul and his soldiers were accustomed to see at Tyre, and going behind the time of Saul we learn with much interest that "the Tyrian civilisation of historic times, so far as we know its actual remains, is little more than a depository of decadent Mycenaean art."[58] We are not, however, aware of anything analogous to the

Phoenician hand having been found by Schliemann; yet it is quite possible there may have been plenty of hands as domestic symbols, though none were deposited in the tombs.

The hands in these illustrations are all "places" such as Saul set up, and the same remark applies to Absalom's "place" in 2 Samuel xviii. 18. It seems a pity, when the meaning is made so plain by these Phoenician trophies, that our eminent scholars who revised the passages did not pause before they translated *jadh* as "place" or "monument." Certainly there was a monument, but it only served as a base whereon was carved the all important symbol—the hand.

How important a position the open hand held in ancient Rome may be seen in the reliefs representing triumphal processions on the columns of Trajan and Antoninus.

The ordinary standard of the Roman legion was anything but a modern flag—it was a true standard, that is, a pole, and, attached to it, was usually a row of round or oblong *paterae*, one over the other; above all, on the top, there were various finials. Some bore a cock, some a very minute banner, the *labarum*, but the commonest top of all was an open hand, sometimes surrounded by a wreath and sometimes alone.

The strange fact is that the Roman eagle, which we should expect to find, is often so conspicuously absent. On Trajan's column, from whence most notions of military accoutrements are taken, there are very few eagle finials compared with hands. More often than an eagle is to be seen a statuette, probably of one of the gods.

In commerce, too, the Romans used the same device. On their weights, particularly on the *quadrans*, the fourth part of the *as* or *libra*, is very frequently to be seen the open hand, with three roundels to show that it contains three *unciae*, each of which differed but seven grains from our ounce avoirdupois; therefore the Roman pound was nearly the same as the modern Italian libra.

Fig. 73 shows one of these weights with an open hand on each side—a right and a left.[59] The club of Hercules which accompanies each of these, is seen on many other of the Roman weights; it is not a

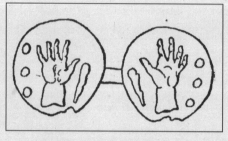

Fig. 73. The Quadrans.

mere decoration, but may be taken with the hand to be of importance, thereby placing the dealer who owned the weight under that hero's protection. Some have a pruning-hook alongside the hand, one of the symbols of Bacchus and of Priapus, both likewise patrons, probably of some other trades using weights, analogous to the *Arte* of Florence, who had each its special patron saint; and just as our modern pawnbrokers mount for their sign the three golden balls of St. Nicholas, their patron.

The open hand, as is well known, was commonly represented as a gesture of angels, and is to be seen thus in the Ravenna mosaics of the sixth century.

In the scene at the church of San Apollinare Nuovo, the angel here shown on the left, Fig. 74, represents but one of a great assembly who hold the right hand thus, in a position which will be instantly recognised as one of the attitudes of benediction still in use, though rather more uplifted, by modern clergy. Our Lord, and the other angel in the illustration, are depicted as making the gesture reserved at present in the Roman Church for the use of the Pope alone; while in other of the mosaics, as in Fig. 75, we find alongside of it the

Fig. 74. San Apollinare, Ravenna.

Fig. 75. San Vitale, Ravenna.

THE HAND

position retained, since the schism of AD 729, as the priestly attitude of solemn benediction in the Eastern Church, as before pointed out, *i.e.* that of extending the index, middle and fourth finger, while closing the thumb and third finger (*digitus medicus*) of the right hand. At Ravenna this attitude is confined to representations of the first person of the Holy Trinity, while the attitude now used by the Pope (called hereafter as the pose of the *Mano Pantea*) is attributed to the second and to the third. In the two scenes in Abraham's life (the offering of Isaac, and the "three men,") placed in juxtaposition, here depicted as if synchronous (Fig. 75), all the three several poses of the hand of which we have been speaking are well displayed. The hand from the cloud and the right hand of the central figure are in the same position, while the right hands of the other persons are making the other two gestures we have been describing. Note the three crossed-cakes, as we have more to say about them.

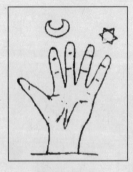

Fig 76. Tunis.

The open hand, moreover, is not only a decorative symbol, as on the great Puerto del Perdon of the Alhambra, upon the Moslem drums of Tunis, Fig. 76 (of which a sketch is here given), as a sign of adoration and also of benediction, but as the symbol of victory on Roman standards and Phoenician "places"; and in all these cases it is well known to be very distinctly prophylactic as well. This is made quite evident by two bronze hands, quite plain and open, but made so as to stand upon their own base, now to be seen at the Ashmolean Museum, numbered 2729, 812 from Jebeil (Byblos). They are both alike in shape, but they differ much in size—one is about four inches, the other seven inches high. It is doubtful whether they are Greek or

Roman work, probably the latter; but a glance at the sketch herewith (Fig. 77) will convince any candid reader that their purpose must have been that of a household ornament, and we doubt not it was considered a protective amulet. In the museum at Zurich is an open hand, numbered 206, of Roman work in terra cotta. It is about natural size, and is precisely of the same sort as the two at Oxford, made to stand upright upon a table. We could not ascertain precisely where it was found, beyond the fact that it was in Switzerland, and that it is an undoubted relic of the Roman occupation of Helvetia. A hand of this kind in so fragile a material is

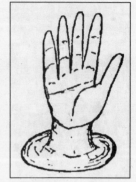

Fig. 77. Ashmolean.

of almost greater value than the same thing in bronze, inasmuch as it goes to prove the common use of these undoubted house amulets, made of mere clay, so as to be within the means of the poor. Their very commonness and easy destructibility fully account for their rarity in terra cotta.

Another large bronze hand of precisely this kind was found at Heddernheim, near Frankfurt, and with a full-sized drawing, nine inches high, is published in a paper by Dr. Becker.

There is an inscription in Roman capitals upon it.

IOVI-DOLICENO
G. IVL-MARINVS
7 BRITTONVM
GVRVEDENS
D D

Without following the discussion as to who this Gaius Julius Marinus might have been, we see here a rare and distinct dedication of the hand to Jupiter Dolicenus, the special divinity of some of the legions stationed in Germania, and we are further interested in the third line. It does not appear where the hand now is, but we pre-

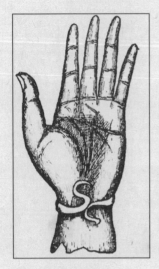

Fig. 78. Kirscherian.

sume in the museum at Frankfurt. This hand bears no mark of having once been the head of a standard.

In the Kirscherian Museum in Rome is another open hand of nearly natural size (Fig. 78), with no other ornament than a sort of conventional snake bracelet. It has apparently been broken off from its stand or base, or per-haps its staff.

In the Naples Museum are two open hands, set on stands; one is quite small, only an inch and a half, the other six inches high, but both are alike in pose, and were evidently house amu-lets. Once more we refer to its analogue as painted on the robe of an American Indian of modern date (Fig. 7). It still continues to be used both on the backs of Neapolitan cab-horses, and as a pen-dant charm *contro la jettatura*, and can be bought in the shops of Naples, made of silver, coral, or mother-of-pearl. There are several open-hand charms in the writer's collection; moreover the Jews use it in this form as an amulet, they have it cut out of flat sheet metal, each side being covered with Hebrew texts, such as, "Hear O Israel, the Lord our God, the Lord is One." A specimen was shown at the Anglo-Jewish Historical Exhibition, 1887, and described to the present writer by his friend Mr. Isidore Spielmann, but there is no photograph of it in the illustrated catalogue, though many other hands in various gestures are depicted; all, moreover, are manifestly intended to be worn as amulets. At Baalbec, in April, 1898, we saw a mendicant Moslem Haji, with green turban, etc., who had on the top of his staff about four feet high a hand of about natural size, cut out of sheet brass, and covered on both sides with Arabic inscriptions. Below the hand the staff was draped with a piece of black muslin. The owner seemed to regard the hand with special care and reverence, nor could he be tempted to part with it.

This was probably that of the Sunni or Arab sect, who, with all Moslems, regard the open hand as peculiarly sacred. Each digit is dedicated specially to, and is taken to personify, one of the holy family. Thus the thumb represents the prophet; the index finger is Abubakr, 1st Kalipha; the middle finger, Umar, 2nd Kalipha; the ring finger, Uthmán, 3rd Kalipha; and the little finger, Ali, 4th Kalipha. The four are called "Chakár Yarán," the four companions (of the prophet).

Among the Shiah or Persian sect the thumb also represents the prophet, while the fingers are:—1st, the Lady Fatima; 2nd, Ali, her husband; 3rd, Hasan; and 4th, Husain, sons of Fatima and Ali.[60]

To sum up, we may accept it as certain that the open hand, whenever depicted, may be taken for the symbol of power and triumph; or, when expressive of an attitude, it is the sign either of benediction or of the extreme reverence of adoration. It may be, as Perrot et Chipiez say (iii. 253), that "la main ouverte et dressée symbolise la prière," and such may be its significance when used as a household amulet. The *lamhdearg*—the red hand of Ulster—is said to be the same as that of the Phoenicians (and we suggest it to be the same as that of the Jews of Jerusalem). The tradition is that it was they (the Phoenicians) who brought it to Ireland, whence, as is well known, it has taken its place in heraldry as the special cognisance of a baronet.

We have dwelt elsewhere, at considerable length, on some other manual gestures, especially those of the Neapolitans, against the *malocchio*, all of which are represented in actual charms, made of various materials to be sold, specially, and avowedly *contro la jetta-*

Fig. 79.

tura. Of these, as shown when treating of hands as charms, by far the commonest is the *mano cornuta*, the position depicted as used by both Dagon and Brahma (Fig. 61), about which it is unnecessary here to say more than that the gesture is known both in pagan and Christian art. The Indian goddess (Fig. 79) in the Somerset County Museum has both hands so posed, and the *Dextera Dei*, in mosaic, on the tomb of Galla Placidia at Ravenna is also in this position; while on other Christian mosaics at Ravenna (as on Fig. 80, St. Luke), the gesture is several times repeated. Hercules is represented upon an ancient Greek vase as the protagonist of a scene. He has a large eye on each breast, and another on each thigh (four in all), very conspicuously drawn. Moreover he is holding up his right hand distinctly in this manner, so that it is evident he was intended to be making the well-known gesture.

On one of the Apulian vases in the British Museum, No. 221 of *cir.* 350 BC is a sitting female, probably Tyche (Fortuna), making this same gesture towards a winged Eros.

The name (*mano cornuta*) by which the hand, with the fore and little fingers thrust out, is known, points to the close connection between it and the all-powerful horns of the several moon goddesses—Ishtar, Isis, Hera, Dinaa, etc.—whose help was supposed to be ever ready to protect their suppliants, and whose horns, the hand thus posed readily signifies. In a former chapter, as well as in another place (*Evil Eye*, chap. vi.), we have dealt with horns at such length that it is only necessary here to refer to the subject.

Fig. 80. San Vitale, Ravenna.

The action of the hands in the pantomimic telling of stories, shown upon many Greek vases, has been also dealt with sufficiently, but it may be here mentioned that several other remarkable ones, told by manual action, are given by Minervini in *Monumenti Antichi Inediti*, Napoli, 1852.

Fig. 81.

Much has been said about that other well-known position of the hand called the *mano in fica*. We have but to repeat that this forms the ordinary silver charm worn with a neck-ribbon by Roman infants of to-day. Fig. 81 is a correct representation from one in the writer's possession. In Naples the children wear the cimaruta, while we used to wear the coral and silver bells; all originally for the same purpose—protection. This *mano in fica*, as we have shown, is the survivor of the *turpicula res* of Varro, and itself was known in classic times as *manus obscaena,*[61] fully described by Ovid. It is this gesture of the hand which is known by all Latin races as *faire la figue,* and expresses the climax of contempt; while in modern Italian, *far la fica* conveys something besides, which is well understood as a *double entendre.* From this comes our common expression, "I don't care a fig." Fig. 82 is from Jorio's *Mimica,* etc., and shows the back of

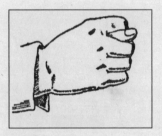

Fig. 82.

the hand in the attitude common in Naples and everywhere else.[62]

Nor is this gesture confined to Europe, for in Batavia (Java) are to be seen two heavy brass guns, in each of which the breech, instead of ending in the usual knob, takes this form. The meaning is fully appreciated by the natives, and the hand in this position is an object of devout worship, especially by childless women.[63]

Besides its many aspects as an instrument for the conveyance of signs and gestures, the hand has always played a very important rôle in all matters relating to magic, divination, or enchantment, and in this connection we cannot overlook the curious belief in "the hand of glory," which seems to have been very widely spread throughout Northern Europe in the Middle Ages, and which is perhaps not yet extinct in parts of Holland, France, Germany, and Spain, while it certainly is still remembered in England. It was "made use of by housebreakers to enter houses at night, without fear of opposition." The true "hand of glory" was the hand of a man that had been hung, which had to be prepared in a very special manner according to a prescription of which a translation has been published by several authors.[64]

The "Nurse's Story" in the *Ingoldsby Legends* is upon the "hand of glory," and begins with three murderers standing beneath the gallows:—

> "Now mount who list,
> And close by the wrist
> Sever me quickly the Dead Man's fist!
> Now climb who dare
> Where he swings in the air,
> And pluck me five locks of the Dead Man's hair!"

On the next page is the description of the old witch preparing the hand for use by a recipe differing from the more authentic one of Le Petit Albert. It runs as follows:—

> "Tis awful to see
> On that Old Woman's knee
> The dead, shrivelled hand, as she clasps it with glee!
> And now, with care
> The five locks of hair
> From the skull of the Gentleman dangling up there,
> With the grease and the fat
> Of a black Tom Cat
> She hastens to mix,
> And to twist into wicks,
> And one on the thumb, and each finger to fix."

The effect of the hand thus prepared is in the main the same as recounted by other romancers.

Its power was believed to be very great, for when set alight at the fingers it held all sleepers insensible and unawakeable within the circuit of its influence. Other accounts say that it stupefied those to whom it was presented, and rendered them not only speechless but motionless, so that they could no more stir than if they were dead. There is some confusion about the several stories told of its wonder-working, but it seems that it had to be lighted at the tips of the fingers, and that so long as it kept burning its effect remained powerful.

Once upon a time, on a dark night, a knock was heard at the door of a solitary wayside inn, and on opening, a wretched beggar, soaked with rain, besought shelter for the night. As there was no other spare place for him he was told that he might lie down before the kitchen fire, which he seemed only too glad to do. When all the household had retired, a maid-servant, who had not liked the stranger's look, determined to watch him, and this she was able to do through a small hole in the door. After a while she saw the beggar get up and go and seat himself at the table. She then saw him draw out of his pocket a black, withered hand, which he set upon a candlestick; he then anointed the fingers and put a light to them. Very frightened she quietly rushed upstairs, but could not wake up either her master or anyone in the house. Creeping back very cautiously she saw all the fingers alight except the thumb—this was because one person in the house was awake. The beggar was collecting all the valuables he could lay his hand upon, but when he had gone into another room, she ran into the kitchen and tried to blow out the burning fingers. Blowing, and pouring the stale beer upon them, only made them burn brighter, and at last, at her wits' end, she caught up a jug of milk and poured it over the hand, when at once the flames were put out, and all the household immediately awoke. The thief was thereupon seized and ultimately hung. There are many stories told of very similar kind, in which it appeared that nothing but milk could extinguish the flame of the "hand of glory."

Old John Aubrey, the Wiltshire antiquary, says it was "generally believed when I was a schoolboy that thieves, when they broke open a house, would put a candle into a dead man's hand, and then the people in the chamber would not awake."

It is said that so late as 1831 some thieves in Ireland entered a house, armed with a dead man's hand, in which was a lighted candle, believing themselves to be invisible, and that it would prevent the sleepers from waking. They, however, failed and fled, but it is evident that the belief was current. Thorp gives a story of a thief in Flanders, upon whom was found the foot of a man who had been hanged, which he confessed was for the purpose of putting people to sleep. There is also another story about some thieves at Huy in Holland who were watched by a maid-servant, and who produced a "hand of glory," but could only make four of the fingers burn, because, as they said, "There must be someone not asleep in the house." They, however, set up the hand with the four burning fingers on the chimney-piece, and while they were gone out to call their mates, the maid rushed in and shut the door against them, but she could not wake the master, until after she had returned, and had at last succeeded in putting out the fingers with milk. In the meantime the thieves were attacking the house, and had just forced the door as the burning hand was extinguished, when of course the men woke up and drove away the robbers. This looks very like a variant of the beggar story, still it is evidence of the widespread belief.

The "hand of glory" was evidently a well-known "property" of the witches and magicians of the Middle Ages. [The Hand of Glory is a tool of sorcery rather than Witchcraft. It requires the dead hand of a hanged man. In days of old, hangings often took place at a crossroads. Hecate, a goddess associated with crossroads, was also one of the witches' goddesses. The fact that witches performed magic at the crossroads may have mistakenly caused people to believe that any magic associated with the crossroads was therefore Witchcraft.] In a very curious picture by Jan Breughel, of which an engraving by Cock is dated 1568, we see his notion of the temptation of St. James—"*Divus Jacobus Diaboliis Praestigiis Ante Magnum sistitur.*" The picture is full of demons of grotesque and utterly impossible shapes, but before a great open fireplace are seated four rats on little three-legged stools, while up the great chimney is flying a witch astride a besom, with another witch coming out at the top;

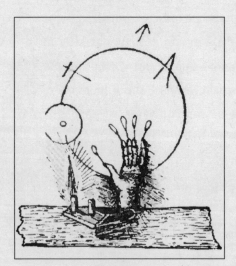

Fig. 83.

but the most remarkable feature of the scene is, that over the chimney beam, known in Somerset as the "clavel," there is fixed a "hand of glory," with a flame rising from every finger.

A later engraving after Teniers, entitled "Depart pour le Sabat,"[65] has many witches, and among other objects, also a large fireplace with a witch riding up the chimney on a broomstick, while again over the "clavel" is fixed a "hand of glory" alight, of which Fig. 83 is a copy.

The original picture of Breughel seems to be remembered by the writer; he believes it to be in the Berlin gallery. The placing of the hands over the chimney by two artists, who were not only not contemporary, but who lived long and far apart, shows the subject to have been quite well and widely understood.[66]

The story of the beggar at the inn is in one place recorded as having occurred in Yorkshire, while substantially the same account is said by Collin de Plancy to be given by Delrio (*Disquisitionum Magicarum*, 1603), but we have been unable to find it after several diligent searches. Those, however, who know the book, will not be surprised at this failure, and the mention of the "hand of glory" by Delrio, together with the part it plays in witch pictures of the Elizabethan period from which we have taken illustrations, show how far-reaching was the superstition. That it lurks even now in many places we may well conclude from its mention by modern authors.

"Thus he said,
And from his wallet drew a human hand,
Shrivelled and dry and black;
And fitting as he spoke
A taper in its hold,
Pursued, 'A murderer on the stake hath died!
I drove the Vulture from his limbs, and lopt
The hand that did the murder, and drew up
The tendon-strings to close its grasp,
And in the sun and wind
Parch'd it, nine weeks exposed.

* * *

The salutary spell
Shall lull his penal agony to sleep,
And leave the passage free.'"[67]

Sir Walter Scott was evidently acquainted with the superstition. In the *Antiquary* (chap. xvii.) he makes the German charlatan Dousterswivel describe it: "De hand of glory . . . is hand cut off from a dead man, as has been hanged for murther, and dried very nice in de schmoke of juniper wood . . . then you do take something of the fatsh of de bear, and of de badger, and of de great eber, as you call de grand boar, and of de little sucking child, as has not been christened (for dat is very essential), and you do make a candle, and put it into de hand of glory."

It is quite clear that the belief as sketched by Sir Walter Scott is a development of the earlier notion of the true "hand of glory." There seems to have been in this as in many other customs a confusion and an overlapping: first the dead hand itself, as we have seen, was to be anointed and set to burn, then a candle made of human fat was to be placed in the dead hand, and later still came the belief still existing that what are called "thieves' candles" can be made from human fat. The conditions as to the hand of a murderer who has been hung, and as to the ingredients and rites to be observed in preparing the hand for lighting, seem to have been dropped, and only the main idea of the human fat has remained.

Though a little outside our subject of the hand proper, a few facts as to this later survival may not be without interest.

In 1619 in Lithuania, a *hausknecht* was tortured with red hot pincers and afterwards burnt alive, on his own confession of several murders, for the purpose of obtaining sinews wherewith to form wicks for "thieves' candles." He also employed the fingers of infants for the same purpose. A cook named Schreiber, at the Castle of Sorau, also confessed to being in league with him, and to having manufactured these candles. At Budissin two murderers were executed in 1602, who admitted that they had committed the same crime.

In 1638 a man was imprisoned for a month at Ober-Haynewald for cutting off the thumb of a man hanging in chains, that he might use it as a "thief's candle." This last example points to the survival of the idea of the original "hand of glory," which the other accounts seem to show had died out.

Frantzen, the Nuremberg executioner, relates in his biography how he had broken on the wheel at Bamberg in 1577 a man who had committed three murders for the sake of the fat of his victims. In 1601 he executed a man guilty of twenty murders, among which were several for the same object—that of making "thieves' candles."

In 1834,[68] in the forest of Plantekow, in Pomerania, an old herdsman, named Meier, was murdered, and on the body being discovered a triangular piece of flesh was found to have been cut from his body, below the heart. The crime remained a mystery for over a year, when a quarrel between the pair led a woman named Berger to denounce her husband as the murderer. Mutual recrimination ended in the arrest of both man and wife, and the story of the latter strikingly accounted for the wounds found upon the herdsman's body. She said that her father had more than once told her husband that the possessor of a "thief's candle" could enter a house and rob it, without those in the house being able to wake so long as it burnt, and that a "thief's candle" was fashioned out of human fat. This idea ran in her husband's head, and he often expressed his desire to have one. She described what he did on the day of the murder, and how on his return he produced the fat he had cut off from under the dead man's ribs, and how they melted it, twisted a wick of cotton, and poured the fat into a mould, but that it would not set, and that it remained fluid and had to be thrown away. The man, who was a known thief, after some time passed in prison, confessed that he had murdered the man at the instigation of his wife and her father, who often told him if they could secure human fat, and make candles of it, "we might rob and steal in any house at night without anyone waking and seeing us."

It came out at the trial that they had borrowed a candle-mould from a neighbour, and also the fact was established that human fat will not set like common tallow in an ordinary mould. The sequel to the story is the strangest part. The man died, protesting his innocence of murder, in 1838. Six years after his execution, in 1844, a sailor was condemned to death in Memel for another crime, and he *in articulo mortis* confessed himself to have been the murderer of the poor herdsman in the wood, and a pouch which he produced was identified as having belonged to the murdered man.

The real connection which Berger, the thief who suffered for it, had with the herdsman, was that by chance he lighted upon the dead body, and the opportunity presented itself to him of obtaining human fat for a "thief's candle." He therefore improved it by cutting out the piece of flesh from under the heart. The story *in extenso* is recommended to the curious.

It is satisfactory to note that except the case mentioned in Ireland in 1831, there have been no recorded instances of this practice in our own country within the present century; but in Central Europe and elsewhere, the belief that certain charms render robbers invisible is evidently still prevalent, and is also the cause of many crimes. Nor does it seem to be peculiar to Slavs or Teutons, for in 1865, in Essequibo, British Guiana, there had been many burglaries, but in no case had the residents been disturbed or awakened by the thief; so that the notion got abroad that the thieves were protected, and could not be caught. A Portuguese, whose store had been repeatedly entered, said, "If lead could not touch them, iron should." He therefore loaded his blunderbuss with broken nails, and hid himself behind his counter. Between two and three in the morning the bolt of the shutter was forced back, and a man got through the window; the shopkeeper fired, and the man fell. On his neck, wrists, and loins were found human bones; he also had others, with some narcotic herbs, which he said he used to make a smoke to cause deep sleep to his victims while he ransacked the premises. He acknowledged having taken the bones from graves.[69] He was a black man, about thirty years of age. He died of the wound. It will not fail to strike the reader that here we have the two old beliefs cropping up—one in the mouth of the Portuguese shopkeeper, that witchcraft cannot stand against iron; and the other in that of a British Guiana negro, about invisibility. The narcotic herbs used by him preserve the ancient notion that fern-seed,[70] and some other vegetable substances, render their possessor invisible.

The virtue of torches made from human fat for other purposes is believed in all over the world.

So late as 1870 a resident in far-off Ningpo relates of one of the Tai Ping rebels, that in order as he thought to discover hidden treasure, he seized the first prisoner he could lay his hands on, and quietly proceeded to cut him up and put him into a large cauldron to simmer until a sufficient coating of oil had collected on the surface;

then a roll of cloth was soaked in this human oil and tightly rolled up into a torch.

The latest account comes from Russia, where, according to a Viennese correspondent, in January, 1889, there was a trial and conviction of four peasants at the South Russian Government of Kursk, for the murder of a girl of eleven, named Lukeria Cherkashina, in October, 1888. Their sole object in killing the child was to make candles, with which they believed they would be rendered invisible, and thereby be able to rob with impunity. It was stated in court that the superstition of "thieves' candles" is still very common in Russia, and it is maintained by Dr. Bloch that it is firmly held by thieves all over the continent of Europe.[71]

In the German criminal statutes of the present century are express penalties against the making of *Diebslichter* or *Schlafslichter*. Even so late as 1876 in Galicia the Public Prosecutor in a murder case referred to the *Schlafslichter*.

Nor has the accusation of murder for the sake of obtaining human oil been confined to thieves. One of the charges made against the Templars was that in their secret rites they took a new-born infant, begotten by a Templar of a maid, roasted it with fire and took all the fat, with which they consecrated and anointed their idol.

The use of the hand in connection with disease such as that referred to by Naaman has been before mentioned, when he expected the prophet to "strike his hand over the place." It is further implied by the name *medicus*, that of the third finger of the right hand; and here again is evidence that a very ancient belief existed in the power of the hand *per se*, and apart from any instrument or medicament.

The king's touch for scrofula was by the hand alone, and being practised so late as the seventeenth century in England shows the extreme vitality of the belief. The strong conviction that there is virtue in the hand of a corpse remains to this day, and here in Somerset it is the commonest thing for a person afflicted with goitre to go to a corpse of the other sex, that the dead hand may "strike" the swelling. In fact this is the recognised remedy.

Aubrey says, "The wenne that grewe in ye man's cheeke at Stowell in Somerset, as big as an egge, was cured by stroking it with his dead kinswoman's hand; and Mrs. Davy Mill (Musitian) had a child with a hunchback cured in like manner."

"For ague, some of the women of Egypt hang to their necks the finger of a Christian or Jew, cut off a corpse and dried."

The power of the "dead hand" is, however, thought to be infinitely greater if the owner had met with a violent death, and above all if by execution of the law.

At the execution of Dr. Dodd in 1777, "after he had hung about ten minutes, a very decently dressed young woman went up to the gallows, in order to have a wen in her face stroked. The executioner, having untied the doctor's hand, stroked the part affected several times therewith."

Many other similar stories may be found in Aubrey, Scott, Brand, and elsewhere, but in these days it will be hardly credited that so late as 1845, at the execution of Crowley at Warwick for murder, scarcely was he dead than the scaffold was crowded with women afflicted with goitre or white swellings in the knee, upon which the dead man's hand was passed to and fro "for the benefit" of the hangman. Whether any benefit accrued to the women does not appear, but the scene described shows the advantage of discontinuing the brutal spectacle of public executions.

The writer well remembers a couple who fixed their wedding for the day of an execution at Taunton, in order that they might go to see the man hung and be married with only losing one day's work.

In Essex so recently as 1895 a female child was taken to be "stroked" by the hand of a dead youth (difference of sex is all important) as a remedy for rickets.

CHAPTER IV.

THE *MANO PANTEA,* OR SYMBOLIC HAND

O F ALL EXPRESSIVE POSITIONS of the hand, certainly the most important, as well as the best known, is that used in the attitude of benediction by the Western Church, but now, for over a hundred years past, limited to the Pope only. Although we have elsewhere devoted a whole chapter to it, the subject is very far from being exhausted.

It was the open hand that was commonly placed upon the top of the Roman standard, as already shown, but the bronze hand in the Naples Museum (Fig. 84 on page 150) is in a different attitude, showing that with which we shall henceforth have most to do. It must have been once mounted on a pole, for we find it prepared by a hollow to take the staff, and there is a hole for a nail to fasten it thereto. The inscription, not to be explained, seems to throw no light on it, but it is, however, probable that this hand found at Herculaneum may have served another purpose; for we know that one of this shape, and with the fingers thus posed, was mounted on a staff, and was formerly carried in France, at coronations, before the

149

king, as *La Main de Justice.* It was preserved in the treasury of St. Denis down to modern times. We may, then, assume this ancient hand to have been part of some civic mace or official staff.

Fig. 84. Naples Museum.

Another hand in this position, found at Pompeii, is in the Naples Museum, No. 5505. It is well moulded, about eight inches high, and being mounted on a plinth, standing upright, is in itself evidence of what we show later on, that the hand alone, posed in this special manner, was an object of much importance and consideration, if looked on simply as a part of the ordinary house furniture.

A hand of this kind appears upon the seal of Hugh Capet, and was in use down to the time of the Renaissance: another example, Fig. 85, is to be seen over the great door of the Cathedral of Ferrara, a building of the twelfth century. We venture to call special attention to this particular hand, because it appears to be placed upon what is well known as the wheel-cross, a very ancient emblem of the sun, and wherever we find it we may surely look upon it as a survival of sun worship.

Fig. 85.

The same object, a cross within a circle, is one of the commonest of brass ornaments seen upon the harness of cart-horses in England and all over Europe, originally so placed, as we show elsewhere, for an amulet against fascination. In Roman times this same sign of the wheel-cross was in very common use; it is shown on several of the pantheistic hands in the following pages, and also on several of the *dischi sacri* in the writer's possession, referred to in Chapter V. The antiquity of this emblem of the wheel-cross, as well as the Oriental source from which it originates, is proved by an example from Nimroud,[72] which shows Baal, the sun god of the Assyrians, posed in front of his own attribute, with his open right hand raised in the gesture already described. The wheel-cross, representing the sun, was, with various modifications, the only object emblazoned upon the shields of many of the Roman legions. Of these we

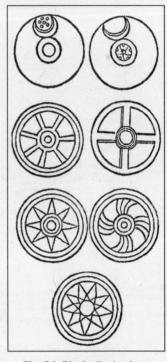

give examples in Fig. 86. Elsewhere we have pointed out that the sun's disc formed the centre of the insignia of nearly every legion of the army of the East; while the disc, or some other symbol of the sun, formed the *umbilicus* of the great majority of those of the West.

It will be noticed that in two of these insignia we have the crescent as well as the sun, while one has the planets in addition.

In Christian times we see it repeated in Ravenna mosaics (see Fig. 74), where our Lord has the same wheel-cross behind his head appropriately and designedly to represent His Godhead; while the angels have but the simple circle or nimbus. Again we see it

Fig. 86. Pincirollo, *Legiones Comitantenses*, xxi. p. 36.

in Fig. 89 *post* where it distinguishes each person of the Holy Trinity. Besides this, its use in mediaeval art will be familiar to every reader.

And, lastly, we find this wheel—this sun emblem—still to be the type of the Irish cross, of many in the Isle of Man, of St. Martin's at Iona, and of a large number in England, many of which are to be found among the crosses of Somerset. We wonder how many of the artists who produce modern pictures of our Lord, and place behind his head a golden wheel-cross as a conventional nimbus, are aware that they are perpetuating an ancient heathen cult, and are demonstrating indisputably thereby, from early and distinctly Gentile sources, His claim to the title of "Sun of Righteousness."

As a confirmation of the assertion that the wheel nimbus in Art was really intended to represent the sun, we give an illustration from

Fig. 87. Giotto, Rosini, ii. 123.

a "Virgin and Child," by Giotto, in which the infant Christ has the cross within the nimbus actually represented by the sun's rays.

It is manifest that Christmas cards and other prints, which place the wheel-nimbus behind the heads of saints, are in error, both historically and mythologically. San Gennaro, on the Neapolitan harness, *inter alia multa*, shown in *The Evil Eye*, p. 204, has a wheel-cross nimbus, but we scarcely look for accuracy among Neapolitan tradesmen. From these facts it is clear that the hand of Justice, backed by the symbol of the supreme Deity, although both elements are essentially pagan in origin, may well be considered appropriate to represent the Almighty, in the second person of the Holy Trinity, in His attribute of Judge. Thus the hand posed as in Fig. 85 takes the place symbolically at Ferrara of the materialistic representations of the last judgment, where He so often appears in person over cathedral doors. In this aspect the wheel-cross is an interesting and undoubted survival of sun worship retained in Christianity.

In Christian art, however, when used alone, the hand in the position we are considering is often depicted with the fingers pointing downwards, and as the *Dextera Dei*, it stands as the recognised symbol of the Almighty Father. It is thus that we find it in so many instances depicted in Miss Twining's valuable book, of which we have already given a specimen (Fig. 71).

Perhaps no example of the hand thus posed, here in England, is more interesting than that on the seal of the Dean and Chapter of St. Andrew's Cathedral, Wells, dating from about AD 1200, which has continued to be used by them, *ad causas*, so late as in the last century (Fig. 88). Another curious fact about this seal is that it bears, along with the *Dextera Dei*, the ancient Gnostic symbols, the sun and moon, on either side of the central figure, just as they are to be seen on many of the gems and seals of the time of the Roman empire, and to be seen to-day on the arms of the old town of Ashburton.

Fig. 88.

Another example of the hand in this position, representing the Almighty power and protection, is in a curious Norman sculpture at Hoveringham, Nottinghamshire, of St. Michael fighting the dragon.

Another is over a doorway at Elkston, Gloucestershire, and one more in Somersetshire on a coffin-lid at Lullington. We have also referred to the same gesture to be seen at Romsey Abbey (*ante*, p. 123). The special position of the hand, with which we are now dealing, when used in sacerdotal benediction, is, however, always more or less uplifted, and not pointing downwards. In mediaeval art this attitude was generally confined to the second person of the Holy Trinity.

It would be easy to reproduce hundreds of illustrations of this

Fig. 89.

attitude, but the reader will notice marked exceptions to the statement given above, for in the early Ravenna Mosaic at S. Apollinare, angels, as well as our Lord are represented in this attitude (*see* Fig. 74).

Again in the very rare fourteenth century MS. in the British Museum, each Person of the Blessed Trinity is represented, but in this case the first and second Persons only are raising the right hand thus; while in Fig. 89 from another fourteenth century MS all three Persons hold the right hand in this position.

We have already seen that this gesture of the hand was well known in Europe and in Asia before its adoption as part of Christian ritual; and yet it is curious that of all the known manual signs used by the demonstrative, half-heathen Neapolitans, this one alone seems at the present day to be tabooed and left entirely to the priesthood, or rather to the Pope.

Canon Jorio, who deals with almost every other manual gesture, leaves this special one severely alone. He never even alludes to it, though his priestly office must have made it to him one of the most familiar of all. How it came to be one of the two adopted attitudes of benediction in the early Christian Church, we cannot absolutely demonstrate, but we can produce very good circumstantial evidence.

That it was well understood in classic times we see clearly from the description of it given by Apuleius.[73] "Porrigit dexteram et ad instar oratorum conformunt articulum, duobusque infimis conclusis digitis, cesteros eminus porrigit." (*Metamorph*. ii. 12.) Probably it was a gesture made by orators in ancient times, but we conclude that it must then, as now, have been held to be a sacred sign. In Switzerland the hand is thus raised to-day, in taking an oath, just as the open hand is among the Jews. We gather this from Herr Meyer's description of the hand (Fig. 106) found at Avenches. He says twice over in his description, "drei finger derselben sind wie zum Schwur erhoben." The plate he publishes shows one of these to be the thumb, and is, in fact, a drawing from the same hand as our own illustrations.

The many specimens of bronze hands, all in this position, which are still preserved, belong to a period anterior to the reception of Christianity in Rome, and the important fact remains, that hands of bronze in this attitude alone of all others, were made the foundation on which to place so many of the attributes of the gods, that they have been truly named Pantheistic. In Chapter V. we hope to show that these hands are a distinct outcome or development of an earlier piling-up of symbols upon a less durable material. It is clear from the number of hands still existing, and from their being always with two first fingers and thumb erect, and also from being always so made as to stand pointing upwards, that great importance must have been attached to the position or gesture itself, apart from the figures embossed upon them. The number remaining, and the general excellence of the workmanship they display, would seem to show that these hands in the first place must be considered to be sacred in character, and next, that they must have played an important part in the daily religious life of the people about the time of the Empire, probably not unlike that occupied by the crucifix of our own days. There can be little doubt but that the *mano pantea*, as it is now called, must have been something much more than a mere household ornament, and we may take it as certain that in Roman families these symbolic hands held about the same position in their day as the figures of the saints and angels, with or without their special attributes, such as those to be found in most southern Italian houses, do at present. They were but a piling-up of the symbols of those particular divinities under whose protection they placed themselves, just as the cross, the heart, the anchor, and other like objects are combined, set up, or worn to-day.

There is evidence that the Romans had many other objects of household or family veneration, besides these hands, although we believe them to have been the most in use. Many such are to be seen in the Naples, Kirscherian, and other museums. One specimen only out of several drawings in our possession comes from the Naples Museum. It was found at Herculaneum, and is manifestly a household ornament. It is of bronze, about six inches in both dimensions. The general shape is a crescent, bespeaking the protection of the Moon goddess. The eagle grasping the thunderbolt appeals to the almighty Sun god, Jove, while the heads on either horn represent probably Cybele on the left and Venus on the right. There is no aperture or any indication of its use for any other purpose than as a domestic ornamental amulet.

If we attempt to analyse the feeling underlying the use of all these symbols, we shall find it to be much the same now as it was then. They remind their possessors of the powerful beings whose protection they seek, or whom they desire to propitiate, but no doubt, then as now, they who used and valued these symbols would as stoutly deny anything like worship of the concrete objects, as their Christian descendants deny that they worship images. They would in both cases profess to venerate (not worship) with the utmost devotion the personages symbolised, whether they be known to them as Barnabas and Paul, St. Joseph and Madonna, or as Jupiter and Mercurius,[74] or Bacchus and Diana. In the one case, however, the objects venerated are to-day called pagan superstitions, in the other religious objects of devotion. Surely we have a survival of this custom in the hand (Fig. 85) over the door at Ferrara.

In seeking to interpret the root idea underlying all symbolism in worship, we must not forget the very narrow border which divides adoration of the image, emblem, or symbol itself, which is idolatry, from that of the being symbolised, which of course, is true worship; the untutored intelligence, however, is but too apt to step over that border, and to confound the one with the other. Of the latter, the uncultured man,

"When the religious sentiment awakens within him, and, at the outset, searches its object and its food in the visible creation, he finds himself face to face with phenomena which he personifies, which are, on the one hand, lovable and loved, as the Aurora, and the life-giving vegetation, with the rain that refreshes and fertilises it; and on the other hand, frightful and terrible, as storm, thunder and darkness. Hence come good gods and evil gods. As a general rule, and in virtue of that naïve egotism which alike characterises the childhood of individuals and of peoples, the dreaded gods are more adored than the loving deities, who always do good of their own account and unasked. This way, at least, the remarks converge of all the voyagers who have closely observed those people of both hemispheres who retain their savage state."[75]

Hence it comes that it is easy to demonstrate how large a place fear has in religion, compared with veneration and love, amongst all primitive peoples; and a little closer investigation, even among a man's own friends and acquaintances, will convince the most sceptical that no amount of civilisation has been able to eradicate it.

We have already shown the gesture we are describing to be one of the sacred sutras of India, and such is the unchangeableness of Orientals, that it probably existed long before Greek or Roman history began. We therefore suggest that this hand posture may always have been held in deep reverence in their ritual by the flamines of old, as representing the *Dextera Jovis*, and thus, having been so shaped in the concrete bronze, may have been subsequently adopted as a suitable base on which to place the symbols of Jove's other attributes, along with those of other gods. And hence we must consider these hands as the classical link between the sacerdotal gesture of Western Christendom and its Oriental prototype, behind which we cannot look. Sittl, in *Die Gebärden der Griechen und Römern*, Leipzig, 1890, p. 325, says that the writing on the wall at Belshazzar's feast (Daniel v. 5) was by a hand, in this position. We have, however, much to say not only upon the hand simply thus posed, but upon the symbols embossed on it, and on their origin.

All the examples hitherto known of the particular kind of hands we are now about to deal with, are either found scattered amongst many museums, or noticed by many different writers, but in no case can more than three or four be found together, either in the concrete or in historical description. Jahn is the first author who has hitherto ventured to bring any number together, and he attempts to portray but two out of the fourteen he enumerates; while the great advantage to students of marshalling the evidence by comparison of the various hands by pictorial means, has never so far been recognised or attempted. He and all the others who have written on the subject seem to have taken for granted that these hands were all votive offerings, but as no arguments have been put forward in support of the assumption, it is here submitted that for this assertion there is but slender authority.[76] It arises, so far as the present writer can discover, chiefly from a single inscription upon one of them, "CECROPIUS V.C. VOTUM S.," *i.e. Cecropius voti compos votum solvit.*

This Montfaucon translates "Cecropius aiant obtenu sa demande a satisfait à son voeu." There is another hand (Figs. 124, 125) now in the British Museum, bearing an incised Greek inscription, showing that it was intended specially to honour Sabazius (the Phrygian

Jove). We have dealt with this at some length elsewhere. Jahn also refers to it as one of the hands known to him. It is, however, one of the poorest examples of which the present writer is able to produce a sketch, and we venture to submit that two inscriptions only upon all the hands known are quite insufficient to build up a confident theory to include the whole. More especially we would remark that there is no evidence as to when this latter hand was engraved, while as to the "Cecropius" hand, the letters are merely upon a separate plinth or stand of uncertain date, and it is even doubtful to which of two different hands the inscription applies.

No other inscription than those above mentioned says anything about a vow. Upon this slight evidence, said to be on one of the best-known hands, published by Montfaucon and by Grevius (*Thesaurus Romanarum Antiquitatum*, xii. 963), and on the doubtful Greek words above referred to, has been founded the conclusion that all these hands were *ex votos* (Jahn cites this hand as *b* in his list). Against this we would point out that the Latin inscription relied upon is, as just stated, simply upon a base, that is not even part of the hand, but is upon a sort of turned plinth, which may or may not have been made at the same time as the hand itself. We should rather conclude that it was made afterwards, and that Cecropius caused the base to be made, to bear the inscription placed upon it, in order to mark that this particular hand was dedicated exceptionally as a votive offering. We understand *votive* to mean something offered in fulfilment of a vow, in gratitude for something received, or vowed as a gift to be made conditionally upon something prayed for being granted. Thus Jephtha's was a true votive offering.

Another fact which seems to tell against these hands being primarily intended as *ex votos* is, that so far as is known, no one of them has ever been found in a temple, or in connection with any statue of a god. On the contrary, they all appear to have been found amongst the ruins of domestic buildings, where lamps, cooking utensils, mirrors, and other bronze articles have been met with.

We place first among our illustrations the specimen best known and most easily examined by our readers for themselves. Figs. 90, 91 represent this hand of Cecropius, known as the Barberini hand, most probably the one now in the British Museum, and called there Payne Knight's. Most of the symbols are identical and in the same position, as on the hand published by Montfaucon from the Barberini collection; Montfaucon's hand, however, has a

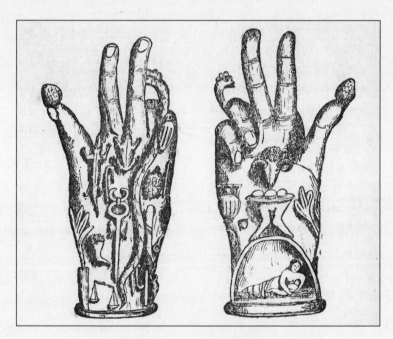

Figs. 90, 91. Payne Knight (British Museum).

third small snake on the thumb, while in it also, the arch over the woman and child is carefully realistic, and is manifestly intended to represent a crescent. There are other differences in the size and moulding of the several objects embossed on each. The fig tree, for instance, in the Barberini, as drawn by Montfaucon, is not, like Payne Knight's, as above, growing out of a stump or trunk; there is, however, a very striking general resemblance between the two, and it is likely the Montfaucon drawing is inexact. We deal with this hand again later on.

It should be noted that the plinth on which the much-becopied inscription was found has entirely disappeared, and it is now extremely doubtful to which of the known hands it really belonged. On the whole it seems most likely that the plinth was made to order with the inscription at a much later date than the hand itself. More-over, as only one or two other known hands bear any inscription at all, it seems reasonable to contend that they were specially made votive offerings, and that being so exceptional they required inscriptions to denote the unusual fact.

A conclusive reason for maintaining that these pantheistic hands were not what they are assumed to be, is that a number of unquestionable *ex votos* still remain, and that from their shape and general condition it is evident that they were intended, like the votive offerings to be seen to-day in modern churches, to be suspended. No doubt many of these latter were in pagan times hung up in the temples near the statue of some favourite god, just as the identical objects are now to be seen hanging near the statue, or in the chapel, of some favourite saint, Montfaucon (vol. ii. plate 100) gives no less than sixteen of these veritable *ex votos* on one large page, and they are precisely such as those with which we are now most familiar—eyes, legs, hands, feet, fingers, etc., but each prepared or pierced for suspension. The only difference is that the modern notion seems to be, to make the *ex votos* represent that part of the body which has been healed by the intervention of the saint, to whom the offering is made; whereas according to many authors, quoted by Montfaucon, each hand, foot, leg, finger, or eye was sacred to and under the protection of some particular divinity; and consequently each member was a symbol of that tutelary deity, and so became a suitable object to be offered by way of gratitude, possibly for favours received, but much more probably for favours to come. Thus we read:—[77]

> "That the eye was consecrated to Apollo, who, according to Plutarch, was symbolised by the Egyptians under the form of an open eye, because the sun, which means Apollo, cast his eye over all the world; wherefore they called the sun the eye of Jupiter, and the Latins called Apollo *Coelispex*, the viewer of the heavens. . . . St. Athanasius says the same, that parts of the human body were adored as special divinities. Some, he says, have placed among the number of the gods . . . the head, the shoulder, the hand, the foot, without reference to the cult of the entire body."

Montfaucon goes on to say that the fingers were consecrated to Minerva. The hand and foot tied together became dedicated to Minerva and Mercury, and the leg with wings on the feet without doubt to Mercury. Altogether the plate is both curious and instructive. From it we give one out of the sixteen examples in Fig. 92.

Fig. 92. Ex voto, from Montfaucon, vol. ii. pl. 100, p. 250.

This account is inconsistent with his remarks upon the ears given in another volume.[78]

"La coûtume d'offrir à Dieu la figure des membres malades, soit pour être delivré du mal, soit en action de graces de la guérison obtenue, cette coûtume, dis-je, est des plus anciens temps."

These ears, he says, were vowed by a person who had been cured of deafness or other *mal d'oreille*; they were vowed in respect of the cure and "non en action de graces."

The whole question of votive offerings is most difficult and obscure, whether viewed as ancient or modern. Probably the ideas which originally prompted them have undergone much evolution, and though the concrete objects survive, many new beliefs may have become encrusted upon them, and yet, *au fond*, remain to-day solid monuments of paganism only half supplanted.

Figs. 93, 94 represent a hand now in the Berlin Museum, but formerly in that of Bellori in Rome. This hand has been more drawn, and is better known to the writers named than any other. It has embossed upon it a bust of Serapis above what looks like a cornucopia, and is perhaps intended for a tripod, of which but one leg appears. But no two drawings are alike, and Jahn (*c* in his list) calls it a bracket. There are also a sacrificial knife, a scarab, and a woman and child under an arch, accompanied by a bird, which seems to be watching them, probably intended for a cock (of which more later), the symbol of the watchful Mercury. On the back is a frog, at the root of the middle finger (*digitus infamis*), a very appropriate position for this well-known aphrodisiac.

The serpent is in this as in other examples also placed with evident design, climbing up the *digitus medicus*, and in combination

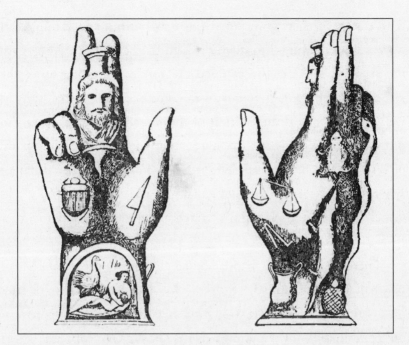

Figs. 93, 94. Berlin.

with it, typifying Æsculapius, the preserver of health; there should, therefore, be naturally a close connection between that finger and the serpent. The balance, *flagellum* (the whip of Osiris), and crocodile, all seem, like Serapis, and indeed most of the other attributes upon these hands, to bear witness to the intimate connection of Roman with Egyptian mythology. This connection would naturally be expected when we consider that the time when these hands were in fashion was just that when the worship of Serapis and Isis had taken firmest root in Southern Italy; when there was the closest mercantile intercourse between its ports and Alexandria. The Serapeum at Pozzuoli and the Iseon at Pompeii are the witnesses. Consequently we find, what indeed we should expect, that the Roman people having already assimilated the Greek Pantheon, would naturally add to it several of the new gods, as well as new notions concerning their own old ones, brought to them through their constant trading with Egypt. Thus it is that we can account for such a piling-up of the symbols of different divinities from countries foreign to Rome, as well as the frequent duplication of the same symbol to be seen in other examples, and also the representation upon the same hand or disc (of which we speak later) of the same divinity by different symbols. These remarks apply equally to the cult of Sabazius and Cybele, Phrygian importations, which became very popular in later Roman times.

There are upon this hand, besides the above, the *cantharus*, or two-handled vase, and the tortoise. We shall have to remark later on upon all of these objects, inasmuch as they will appear in various combinations over and over again. The extreme conservatism of popular habit and belief is well exemplified by the fact that we are able to show, by specimens in the writer's own collection, that nearly every one of these symbols survives to-day, alone and separated from the rest, as well as combined with many others, as an amulet, made and sold in the shops for a *porta fortuna*, that is, against the evil eye. They are often to be seen in shop windows, labelled *contro malocchio* or *contro la jettatura*.

It is this particular hand which has been carefully imitated by Roman silversmiths and sold as a revival of an ancient amulet against *malocchio*. Two of these, one mounted as a pendant, the other as a brooch, are in the writer's collection of modern charms. These hands are said to have been used as *amatoria*, and at the same time they are called *votive*. The scarabaeus upon Fig. 93 shows its intimate connection with Egypt, where it was a symbol of the renewal of life or resurrection, as well as of the path of the sun (who dies and rises again daily)—a notion derived from the creature's well-known habit of rolling round balls of clay with such persistence. Dried beetles, powdered and mixed with wine, were considered, according to Pliny, to be an infallible *amatorium*. The scarab in this case is placed over the woman and child, wherefore it is said to represent simply the phenomenon of generation. This same notion is repeated by the *flagellum*, the whip of Osiris, which will be found on many of these hands; moreover, it is here, and in the next hand we have to deal with, placed immediately over the *cantharus* or two-handled vase, one of the recognised symbols of Osiris, the god whose story is so intimately connected with the Nile. Other authorities make the whip the symbol of Bacchus.

The *flagrum* or *flagellum* of Osiris was the restorer of virile power, and according to Apuleius was the proper sign for a seminator.[79] It was, moreover, the symbol of divination, and may also bear reference to the *Lupercalia in ludo Junonis*, which latter goddess was believed to be the same as Isis herself. On the other hand Montfaucon says that the whip is a sun sign, that it represents Apollo (Phoebus), for with the whip he urged forward the horses of the sun. This view is but the classic dress of the older Egyptian myth of Osiris in his aspect of a sun god.

The entire hand manifestly symbolises Serapis, who really is the same as Osiris (*Osiris-Apis*), and we may expect every symbol upon it to be in some way connected with or related to him or to Isis.

Returning to the first illustration, Figs. 90–91, drawn from the original now in the British Museum. It is part of the collection of the late Rev. Payne Knight, but it is not known how or whence he obtained it. We must, however, consider it to be the same as that depicted with the inscription by Montfaucon, vol. ii. pi. 137, (p. 330), and by La Chausse (Causseus) said to have been in the Barberini collection. As will be readily observed, it is a most interesting example, containing a much greater number of attributes than Figs. 93–94, which has thirteen while this has twenty-five. Of these, several are the same on both hands here illustrated, while some others are but alternative symbols of the same divinities. Here, instead of the bust of Serapis, we have the ram's head, which generally represents Mercury, to whom we must conclude this hand more especially to appeal. We often see the head of Serapis on coins and gems (*e.g.* Fig. 3) with curled ram's horns, which, as we show elsewhere, are different *toto coelo* from those of the goat; but the entire ram's head seems not to have been one of his symbols.

The ram is here appropriately placed upon the *mons Jovis*, the root of the middle finger, which in all cases we must take to be the place of honour on every hand, and evidently represents the god to whom the hand is sacred. Immediately beneath is the tripod bearing the three cakes, a common sacrificial offering. Again, this is immediately over the woman and child, so that we may in this case safely consider the ram's head of Mercury to represent the same set of ideas as that conveyed by the scarab; the cakes typify the divinity of the being to whom they are supposed to be offered, in the same way as in the other hand this is signified by the sacrificial knife. The *cantharus*, again, being above the woman, implies that she is under the protection of Dionysos or Bacchus, the generative power. Other writers, as before noted, make the *cantharus* to symbolise Osiris.

The tripod is an altar of sacrifice, and hence also denotes that a deity is above it.[80] Taken alone the tripod is said to represent Time—past, present, and to come. It is also said to represent the divine Triad of pagan antiquity. Mr. Frazer says there is much difficulty and confusion regarding tripods—that they were dedicated to Apollo at Amyclae, to Hercules at Thebes, to Zeus at Ithome—and he remarks upon the contest of Hercules with Apollo for the tripod. On the whole, he considers the dedication to have been to Apollo. There was once a street in Athens named "Tripods."

We must not omit again to point out the striking analogy of the three cakes, which occur again and again, not only upon the hands, but oftener still upon the earlier *dischi sacri*, and, as we have shown elsewhere, upon the altar of Melchisedek, and before the three strangers entertained by Abraham, from the early Christian mosaics of Ravenna (see Fig. 75). Cakes were offered in the Erechtheum at Athens to the supreme Zeus.

The pine-cone mounted on the thumb appears on this and several other hands, and we always find it in a conspicuous place, showing it to be an important attribute of whatever god it symbolised. We find that it was sacred to Serapis, and also to Cybele, and being on the thumb, believed to be the seat of power in the hand, we may take it to imply the god's might, apart from his sensuality. The pine was the tree of knowledge in its Chaldean name *asnan*, and in Babylonish, *asnan* meant also pine-cone. The Romans called the pine, *pura arbor*; it was beloved by girls, and hence at Rome a type of virginity, so that they may well have engrafted the Oriental significance of the cone upon their own tradition. As with the tripod, so with the pine-cone, there is much uncertainty and difficulty. It is pointed out by Mr. Marindin that the pine tree was sacred to Atys, and in the Megalesia, the festival held in honour of Cybele, who was worshipped with Atys, it was carried in procession. As we find Cybele certainly to be represented prominently on other hands, *e.g.*, Fig. 103, we may perhaps conclude the pine-cone to be her symbol, but in view of modern usage of it, this is not to be taken as decided.

As a modern amulet the pine-cone is very common. Especially is it set up for a protection to vineyards, gardens, and entrance gates generally. Along the new Cornice Road, from Positano to Cetara, past Amalfi, the pine-cone in terra-cotta, red and new, may be seen on the piers and walls of numberless new vineyards and orange terraces, constructed to supplant the olives, now being rooted out.[81] It is not placed as a mere finial, but is manifestly for a purpose well known. In the Vatican Museum are to be seen no less than four large pine-cones set on handsomely carved dwarf columns, in all about six feet high, of fine white marble, and evidently intended to stand alone just like a statue or other object of art. The columns are all different in design, though each is evidently meant to bear the pine-cone as its chief attraction, while the elaboration with which the capital of each is carved, proves the great importance of the symbol it bears. The whole thing is such as can only have been suitable for the grandest of Roman palaces.

According to Lazard, the pine-cone had also a phallic significance, and was much used in the cult of Venus, but we may dismiss that consideration of it here. Its use in gardens and vineyards seems rather to point to Bacchus or Priapus, the patron deities of vineyards, but probably on these hands the Phrygian Cybele is the deity symbolised.

The crocodile or lizard, for they seem to be taken as one and the same symbolically, has been dealt with at some length elsewhere. It was thought to be the type of silence, and to denote both the wisdom and the silence of the wise. This idea arose, according to Pliny, from the fact(?) that of all land animals the lizard and crocodile are without tongues.

A lizard mounted as a modern amulet is quite common in many lands. It is made in painted porcelain at Caldas in Portugal, to be affixed to a wall, and it is manifestly intended as a house amulet. We have elsewhere alluded to the Lagarto suspended over the door of Seville Cathedral since 1260, also to the crocodile upon which stands St. Theodore at Venice, and refer the reader to the remarks generally thereon, to which, if space permitted, much might be added. Even the Moslems of Tunis and elsewhere still set up a crocodile over their doors. We have seen one with a horse-shoe on its tail and another on its snout, of course to enhance its power.

Seeing that we are now dealing with the objects on the back of the hand, we may, perhaps, consider them to be the attributes of other deities than the great ones typified upon the more important positions on the palm and thumb, to whom principally the hand was dedicated as an object intended to stimulate veneration. We find, then, that both lizard and tortoise were sacred to Mercury, and as we see that the caduceus, his undoubted symbol, is placed between them, we may accept it as certain that Mercurius Triceps, in his threefold attributes, is here intended. Fig. 95 (on page 172) is from Liceto, and the same representation is to be found in Calmet's *Dictionary of the Bible*. Later we have more to say on this figure of Mercury.

Next we find the frog in the same position as before, and doubtless having the same signification, about which we have said sufficient elsewhere; but being here placed between the lizard and tortoise, directly over the caduceus, we must take it that Mercury is typified in his sensual attribute, for he was one of the four lascivious gods with Liberus, Priapus and Phallus. He was worshipped as such under his Greek name Hermes, and hence the obscene statues called Hermae, which, in one respect, were always considered to be set up as prophylactics against fascination.

Fig. 95. Mercurius Triceps.

The two whips also in juxtaposition, together with the two serpents in erect position, lend to the entire group a quite unmistakable meaning. The large protecting serpent climbing up the *digitus medicus* and looking out over the front of the hand, along with the smaller one climbing up the index, have a twofold meaning. As representing Æsculapius, we suggest that they typify a prayer to that god for preservation in health, specially as regards the cult of Hermes; while the erect posture marks the serpent as the watchful guardian, to be seen especially on each side of the entrance of tombs, whether rock-hewn, as in the tombs of the kings at Thebes, or as at Gavr Innis in Brittany, or on many a cinerary model house, in which the Romans placed the ashes of their dead. Many of these latter are to be seen in the Vatican, Florence, and other museums, having a Medusa's head on the door, and an erect serpent on either post.

We have suggested elsewhere that the cable mouldings on windows and door jambs, so common in Venetian architecture; also twisted columns in the like position, to be seen in many other places, are but the conventional representation of the protecting serpent Agathodemon.[82] We cannot forget that the chimaera itself represented a combination of the three great forces of Nature—the generator, the preserver, the destroyer—by the goat's head, the serpent for tail, the lion for body.

It is doubtful whether the insect perched on the serpent is a bee sacred to the Ephesian Diana, or a cricket; both were powerful amulets, dealt with elsewhere. On further examination of this hand (Figs. 90, 91) we find that lower down, at the back of the wrist, are the attributes of other deities. The fig tree was the symbol of Priapus, the cornucopia of Ceres and Fortuna (Greek Tyche). The thyrsus and vase were the representatives of Bacchus, the vase of Osiris also; while the two flutes were peculiar to Cybele, the curved, or Phrygian flute, denoting the Phrygian cult of that goddess in Italy. The balance which appears on this and on many other hands is not to be easily explained. Otto Jahn plainly says he cannot do so, nor can the present writer do more than suggest that it may have been inserted as a type of justice, intended to appeal generally to the gods propitiated under their several attributes. Schliemann (*Mycenae and Tiryns*, p. 199) found two golden balances in one of the tombs, but offers no suggestion or explanation as to their meaning. Many of the objects found were protective of the dead, and seeing how often the balance occurs on these hands, we cannot but conclude that it had some important symbolic meaning. There is one other symbol on this hand, which is by no means uncommon, that cannot be explained with any confidence. It is a kind of horse-shoe ending in two rings or bows. We found an amulet for suspension in the Etruscan Museum at Bologna which is much like it. Provisionally it is suggested to represent a pair of *crotala* or cymbals, sacred to Cybele. Taken altogether this hand must be looked upon as mostly lascivious, with a few attributes appealing to nobler qualities, such as the bee, the tripod, the balance, and the flutes, thrown in.

Fig. 96 is a sketch taken direct from another very interesting example. It was found at Resina, *i.e.* Herculaneum, in 1746, and is No. 5506 now in the Naples Museum.

If any further argument were needed to prove that these hands were not *ex votos*, as generally understood, it is furnished by this exam-

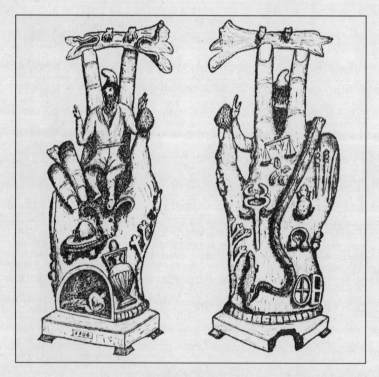

Fig. 96. Herculaneum.

ple. The stand with four feet, on which it rests, is part and parcel of the same bronze as the hand itself. It was therefore manifestly intended to stand alone, on a flat surface, and could not have been suspended or mounted on a staff. Among the twenty-nine objects upon this hand is the full figure of a man, an object quite unique as such, although there are several heads on other hands, of the same bearded personage. From the prominence given to him, he must represent one of the greater gods, and from his cap and dress, which are distinctly Phrygian, he must be Sabazius, about whom we read, that he was a Phrygian deity "whom the Greeks identified with Dionysos and sometimes also with Zeus." His orgiastic worship became widely spread in later times throughout Italy. We find that the snake was his special symbol, scorpions also were sacred to him, and he became identified with Jupiter in his lower animal attributes. The Sabazia in Greece were festivals of so licentious a character that, at the time of Demosthenes, it was not considered respectable to take part in them. We can further identify this figure by the solid-looking thunderbolt across the fingers above his head on which are two snakes, his own symbols; while perched in its proper place, grasping the thunderbolt, though now of course broken off and gone, was Jove's own eagle. This we see by the claws which alone remain on this and several other hands.

At his feet are the ram's head, the tripod and offering, on which we have already remarked, denoting his divinity, and beneath, on the wrist, are the same woman and child, with the *cantharus*. On the back we find nearly similar objects to those on Figs. 90–91, though disposed somewhat differently; the serpent, the snake, and pinecone, however, are in nearly the same places, the snake on the *digitus medicus* in both cases.

Beneath the balance are four leaves crosswise, which we cannot explain, although the same symbol appears on the Tarentine *dischi sacri* (*post*). There are two knives, two frogs,[83] and but one whip. The cymbals or *crotala* represent Cybele, the *mater deorum*; and below is the wheel-cross, a sun sign, which we have already discussed. The oblong with two holes and the object above it cannot be identified, notwithstanding that this is one of the best-finished hands the writer has seen. The minuteness of the objects (for the entire hands are somewhat smaller than natural size) is such that, poor as are the drawings, they are more distinct than on the bronze originals. The uplifting of both hands by Sabazius in the special pose has its significance.

Fig. 97 is from the original, numbered 595/384 in the Naples Museum. It was found in 1894 in Pompeii, and has not before been published. In general size it is about the same as the rest; all are from five to six inches high in their present mutilated condition, *i.e.* with the eagle gone. The average size is well typified by the three or four specimens in the British Museum. This hand again had Jove for its chief deity, though he is only indicated by the tripod with offering cakes, and by the thunderbolt with feet of the eagle, the body of which has in all cases disappeared. The fractures are quite plain in the original bronzes, and the claws show that the bird always faced to the front of the hand. Here again the woman and child are guarded by a cock, and in this case, being somewhat more distinct, it helps to identify the bird.

The cock was sacred to several divinities among the Greeks; to Athene (Minerva) and to Ares (Mars), on account of his pugnacity, hence at Athens cock-fighting was instituted during the Persian War. He was sacred to Apollo,[84] to the Sun, and to Æsculapius.

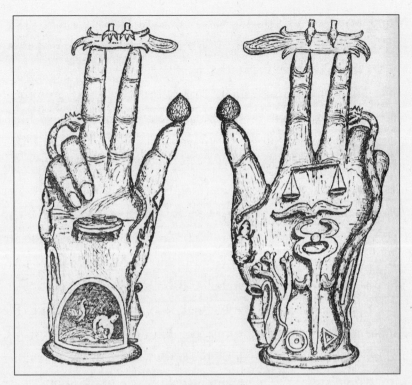

Fig. 97. Pompeii.

The cock was the patron or symbolic cognisance of ancient Imera, in Sicily, said to have been so adopted as representing Æsculapius, the god presiding over the hot medicinal springs. Those of Imera were celebrated throughout Sicily, Greece, and Italy, and their fame amounted to a religious cult, to such an extent that among the Greeks it developed into a worship of mineral springs generally. Heckhel believes that the cult of Æsculapius arose at Imera, of whom the cock was the symbol. Hercules is also said to have been the founder of the baths of Imera, and that the cock was also his symbol. Another account is that, as the herald of the dawn, he is called ημερόφωνος, and that from the similarity of sound the people of Imera placed him upon their coins. On the other hand,

Montfaucon says that the cock was sacred to Mercury. All this does but confirm the almost inexplicable confusion of ancient mythology, to which we have so often to refer.

On the back of this hand Mercury takes again the prominent place with his caduceus, above which are a bow and the usual balance. The bow is difficult to explain with certainty, for not only Diana and Hercules are often shown carrying a bow, but Juno Martialis has one as well, in some statues, according to Montfaucon. The disc, or *patera*, at the foot of the fig tree is said to denote the earth, and thereby Cybele or Vesta, who were its tutelary deities. The snakes, as before stated, we believe to represent Sabazius, the Phrygian aspect of Jove. The one-handled ewer is a symbol of Bacchus the wine god.

It has been suggested that the snakes on these hands point to the double connection of the "genius loci" with the earth and its fruits, and the underworld of the dead; but it seems improbable that along with symbols directly representing definite personifications there should be any denoting a mere abstraction. All the symbols are surely direct appeals to special deities. It is possible, however, that they may on these hands symbolise the tutelary deity or "famulus genius loci." "Geniumne loci famulumne parentis." (Virgil, *Aen.* v. 95.) Moreover, we can only explain the balance as a symbolic abstraction.

The triangle, like the cymbals or crotals, was also, as a musical instrument, one of the symbols of Cybele and therefore we may consider her to be intended by it. Several meanings were implied by a triangle. According to many writers of the phallic school, it represented the female principle in nature. Others say that it represented the threefold nature of the gods, implied respectively in *tria virginis ora Diana, Diana Triformis, Mercurius Tresmegistus, fulmen trifidum* of Jupiter, the trident of Neptune, etc. Others again declare it to represent the perfect, magical, and mystic number three, but all associate it in some way or other as a sign expressive of divinity. An object on the front of the thumb and another on the wrist cannot be identified.

Another hand, Figs. 98–99, is also sketched from the original, now in the museum at Brescia, recently discovered in a field near the city, but far from the temple. It also has never before been published, and so far as one could ascertain on the spot, neither it nor its companion, found about the same time, have ever until now excited any tourist's or other attention. The Curator seemed surprised to find anyone to take interest in such things. Here Jove is denoted by a wheel-cross as the sun-god, while the ram's head is mounted on the third

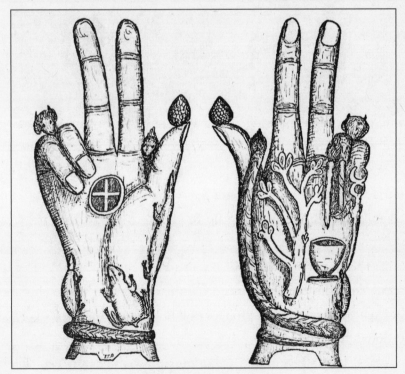

Figs. 98, 99. Brescia.

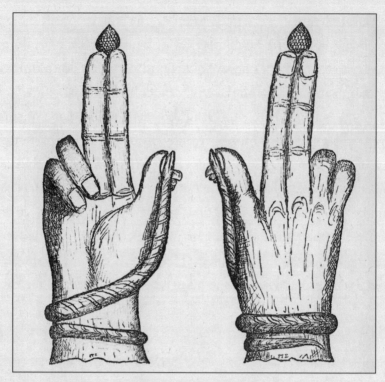

Figs. 100, 101. Brescia.

and fourth finger, a position it occupies on other examples. The frog and tortoise on the front of the hand instead of the back are unusual; so are the cup without handles, and the torch on the back. Next to the latter is the common straight flute. The large serpent, here twined about the wrist and climbing up the hand, is looking out between the thumb and index. It will be noticed that the large serpent is like other specimens hooded, and that this hand is also cast with feet to stand alone. In several respects it is quite unlike most others, but the differences themselves are proof of careful design in the disposal of the various attributes.

Figs. 100–101 are from the original now also at Brescia, which was found near, and about the same time as the last described, but is

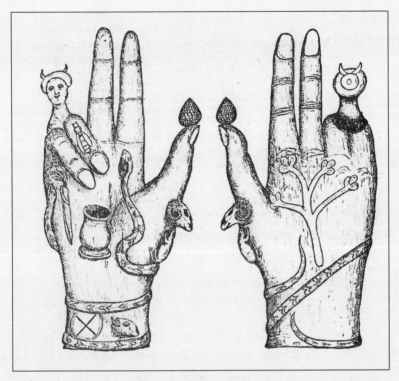

Figs. 102, 103. Louvre.

in a much worse condition through corrosion. It is, however, quite plain that it never had more figures upon it than are now drawn—the serpent and pine-cone, which latter in this case occupies an unusual place on the finger-tips, where hitherto has rested the thunderbolt. The hooded serpent too, although connected with the thumb, is differently placed to any we have so far noted.

Figs. 102–103 are from the original hand in the Louvre Museum, and never before published. It is difficult to discover any special meaning to this hand, which, by the way, is not in a good state of preservation. Besides three or four of the old familiar symbols, we have a head perched upon the bent joints of the third and fourth fingers, but it is not quite certain whom it represents. Seeing, however, that we have an undoubted Mercury in this same position on two other hands (Figs. 107, 113), it is tolerably safe to conclude that it is intended for him, and that the little points on his hat which look like horns are really meant for wings. The wings of Mercury on Fig. 107 are almost as ideal as these. The smooth face, too, and the round hat both point to him, although Seyffert says that Sabazius was often represented with horns, but then he is generally bearded. The torch on this hand is unmistakably seen only on one other (Fig. 99). For the first time we find a goat's head on the wrist, as well as a ram's on the thumb; this is of course to represent Pan. The two large serpents on the same hand are quite unique in our experience, and moreover these are not crested. We note here also the *crater* without handles, as in Fig. 99.

Next to Jupiter, under his various aspects, Mercury must certainly have the second place upon all these hands, and like Diana, as explained elsewhere, he has a trinity of attributes. Fig. 95 shows "Mercurius Triceps," often in company with Serapis and Isis; "nam Mercurius et terrestris, et celestis vocatus fuit, quod illi accidit vel propter triplices vires, quas obtenebat, naturalem scilicet moralem, et rationi obtemperantem facultatem, vel quod cum congressis, tres filias suscepisset."[85] He is also called "Mercurius Tricephalus," *i.e.* he is a god in heaven, earth, and sea (Giraldus). Servius, quoting Cicero, says he is Tricephalus, because some Hermae are made *tricipites* in order to point the way in three directions. "Mercurius Tresmegistus appellatus quod nunc fuerit simul et Maximus Princeps, et Maximus Sapiens, et Maximus Sacerdos."[86] On the heads of the figure of Mercurius Triceps (Fig. 95) are three lilies, the royal flower, the flower of Juno; in the two hands are burning two lamps, these represent will and intellect. Can these be any other than the pagan prototypes, adopted into the Christian Church? These two lights were pronounced to be lawful in the Anglican branch by the decision recently (July 31, 1899) given by the two archbishops.

There are in the Louvre two other of these hands. They are smaller than usual, and so much corroded that it was not possible to make satisfactory sketches, but we noted that one of them was remarkable in having a pine-cone, not only on the thumb, but also on both tips of the upright index and middle fingers, three in all. There was a tripod and three snakes on the hand, two climbing up the thumb and one at the side of the palm, while as usual Agathodemon was looking out from behind over the *digitus medicus*.

The third hand in the Louvre, which there was no opportunity to sketch, is much smaller than most of those known to the writer, though it must have been finely executed. The thunderbolt, with eagle's claws remaining, is on the tips of the fingers; there are also a ram's head and two serpents, but the other figures are so indistinct as not to be made out. The backs of both are too much damaged to attempt description, but they probably had some of the usual symbols.

Figs. 104–105 (page 184) are from the original in the Kirscherian Museum in Rome, never before published. There is nothing unusual about this hand, except that it is not so well modelled as most others. The symbols seem to point to several separate deities, rather than to the elaboration of the attributes of one or two in particular. The prominence of the ram's head makes this also a Mercurial hand, while Mercury, Priapus, Æsculapius, Bacchus, are clearly represented by the usual symbols before discussed, and perhaps Venus also by the frog.

The ears on this ram's head are so erected as to appear like a second pair of horns. Compare this with the Egyptian god Chnemu

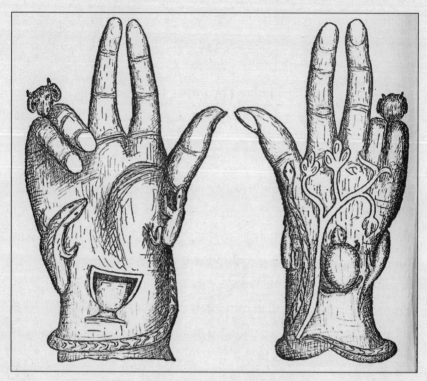

Figs. 104, 105. Kirscherian.

referred to (p. 12). It is strange that we can find no one personage
in the Roman pantheon whom we can certainly describe as represented by either the frog or the crocodile. On both Pliny descants
at considerable length, and inasmuch as we find one or both upon
the majority of these pantheistic hands, we must conclude that
they were like the balance, intended to reinforce certain attributes
of the gods symbolised, or possibly to represent special qualities
to be aimed at in the daily cult wherein we believe these hands
held their place. The extreme licentiousness of Roman society in
the later period to which these hands belong, lends consistency to
the belief that Aphroditic worship is, to a great extent, symbolised
by them. It is probable that as symbols both frog and crocodile

HORNS OF HONOR

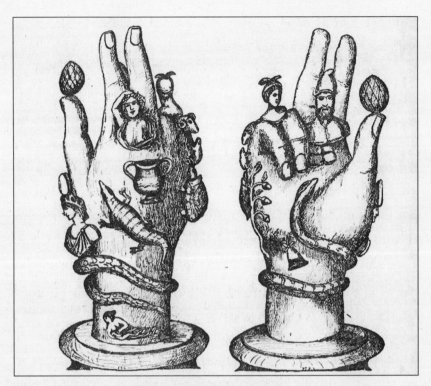

Figs. 106, 107. Zurich Museum.

came to Rome with Serapis from Egypt, and that as both creatures were held there in great reverence, so they took a like place
in the estimation of the Romans. It is certain that the frog has
maintained its position down to the present time, for it is still one
of the commonest of modern Italian and Greek amulets; like the
lizard and tortoise it is also made at Caldas as a Portuguese amulet.
The writer possesses frog amulets from Constantinople, Smyrna,
Athens, Naples, and Rome.

Figs. 106–107 show a hand now in the Museum at Zurich. It
was found in 1845 at Avenches in Canton Vaud, near the lake of
Morat. Aventicum was once the Roman capital of Helvetia, and thus
no explanation is needed to account for the find. The illustration is

from the original, though a plate of it is given in Herr Meyer's article. This example is mentioned by Jahn, but he only quotes Meyer, and the drawing of the hand was not published by the latter till 1856, after Jahn wrote. The writer had an opportunity of comparing Herr Meyer's plate with the original, and has ventured to put forward his own sketch here given from one taken on the spot, as a little more correct in detail.

Herr Meyer follows the old story as to this being a votive hand, and assumes that this was one made by a *Wöchnerin* for a safe delivery; but although he produces no evidence except the presence of the woman and child in support of this; he himself furnishes, in his description of another hand, almost certain proof that such was not the intention of one at least of them; and arguing from the known to the unknown, we again confidently submit that not any one of them was an *ex voto* at all, *i.e.*, for favours received, but rather an expression of supplication to the gods for blessings to come. On the hand in the Zurich Museum (Fig. 106), he seems to support our contention, for he remarks, that it is not improbable the mother depicted may be seeking the protection of the deities for her new-born child, and by the aid of powerful amulets to guard it from sorcery and witchcraft. He says that in the Leyden example (see *post*, Fig. 120), on the other hand, instead of the woman and child upon the wrist (where, in all these hands known to us, they alone are placed) there stand the man and wife together, holding each other's hands over an altar. "Who can doubt that this represents an appeal to the divinities shown above them for a safe and happy delivery to come?" Here we entirely agree with him. On this Meyer, who is not very clear, goes on to say, that it is also an *ex voto* for a safe delivery, "wie O. Jahn sagt," showing, as we submit, that Meyer does not himself quite believe it, though he does not venture to controvert so great an authority as Jahn.

It cannot be reasonably maintained that the same object can be intended as a propitiatory or protecting amulet, and at the same time be an *ex voto* or thank-offering in fulfilment of a vow, conditional upon the favours prayed for having been received. Meyer says of the Avenches hand (Fig. 106) that it excels all others in the richness and multitude of the objects upon it, and in this also we agree with him. It is undoubtedly sacred to the Phrygian god (Sabazius), who had in the later period of the Empire almost entirely engrossed the worship of the Roman people to the exclusion of Jove in his other aspect as Serapis. From its delicacy of workmanship, and the tenderness (*weichheit*) of the fingers, he considers it to be a woman's hand, and he compares it unfavourably with the patched-up and new hands upon many of the antique statues, very few of which have been found with their fingers perfect. He says it is about four inches high, and it rests upon a round base. We say it is nearer six. On the thumb is a pine-cone, and on the bent third and fourth fingers is a head of Mercury, young, and with wings on his cap. On the back, behind the fore and middle fingers, is a bust of Bacchus, holding his hand over his head, which is decked with grapes and vine leaves, while his breast is partly covered by the *chlamys*; behind Mercury is a ram's head. The bust on the front of the fore and middle fingers is the Phrygian Sabazius, the same bearded face we see in Figs. 96 and 108. His cap is of the usual type, but with two projections, which perhaps represent the horns with which he is so often depicted. The objects immediately below him are probably intended for offering-cakes, as seen beneath Serapis in other hands, except that here are four instead of the usual three.

Close to the ram's head is the frog, and next to him the tortoise, then the *cantharus*, and next the crocodile. On the root of the thumb is the bust of Cybele, wearing the turret crown, and over her head the *tympanum* (prototype of the tambourine), one of the proper attributes of this Asiatic goddess. The serpent on this hand differs from most others, in twining twice round the wrist and then climbing up the palm instead of the back of the hand. This occurs in Fig. 102, now in the Louvre. Near the serpent is a cap surmounted by a cross, and then a branch of oak, having exaggerated acorns. On the front of the wrist is the woman and child, but without the usual arch over them. Altogether this is a most interesting hand, from the number of busts of deities upon it. The other objects, except the cap and oak branch, are common enough. The strange mixing up of all these gods, the Phrygian Sabazius and Cybele, the Romano-Greek Hermes or Mercury, Dionysos or Bacchus, with the Egyptian crocodile and serpent, bear witness to the effect which the conquered people had upon their conquerors, and proves the readiness of the Romans to adopt any religion, or even none at all, from those with whom they were brought into contact; indeed, had they been now existent, they would well deserve the name "undenominational," from comprehending all while preferring none.

Figs. 108–109 are from Caylus (Tubières) *Recueil*, vol. v. pi. 63; in Jahn's list, p. 101 (*g*). This hand is remarkable from being a left hand, the only one of this kind known to the writer, a fact unnoticed hitherto, and it is clear from this out of many oversights, that Jahn and others who have written upon them have

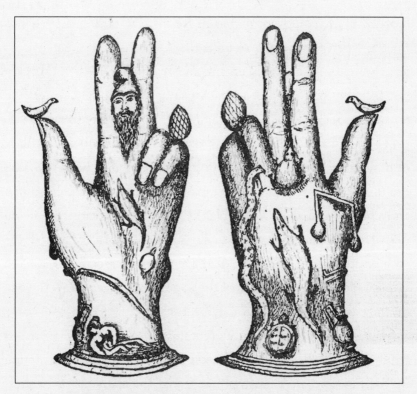

Figs. 108, 109. Caylus (Tubières) *Recueil*, vol. v, pl. 63.

not given these important objects very close examination or attention; they have for the most part merely quoted from each other or copied from others. The head here is evidently the same as that of the figure in the same position on Figs. 96, 107. From his cap we believe that he represents the bearded Phrygian Sabazius, which we must take from his repeated appearance to be proof of his having at least rivalled, even if not supplanted, both Serapis and Jupiter in the Roman pantheon. It has been suggested that this bust may be that of Mithras, whose cult, though brought to Rome by Pompey, was very much in vogue under the later Empire: yet we submit that he is always represented as a smooth-faced youth, and therefore the bearded figure could not be meant for him. We think these hands for the most part belong to an earlier period, seeing that two, at least, were found at Herculaneum and Pompeii, and therefore cannot be later than AD 60, when Mithraic worship had scarcely so far taken root as to have supplanted Sabazius. Moreover, Fig. 96, probably one of the earliest, has Sabazius undoubtedly in the place of honour. It is hard to say what bird is intended to be perched on the thumb, probably the dove, an attribute of Venus. The woman and child are in their usual place, but are remarkable for being placed under the snake or smaller serpent instead of under the arch or crescent.[87] Moreover, we have here two crocodiles, as if to impose silence on both sides of the hand. The object below the one on the palm is uncertain, it may be a scarab.

Figs. 110–111 are from the museum of St. Geneviève, and this hand was published by Montfaucon (vol. ii. pi. 137). It was found in Tournay, and after having disappeared for many years, its present resting-place is the usual bourne of lost antiquities, the British Museum. The front only of this hand has been hitherto published, first by Pignorius, from whom Montfaucon copied. The present writer is now able for the first time to supply the deficiency from a sketch made from the original, and so to exhibit this hand like the rest front and back. Bacchus is strongly represented by the two thyrsi, while the crescent upon the palm is quite a new feature, representing Diana according to all authorities. The two round caps are said to represent Castor and Pollux, and the cross on the top of each their respective stars. On the back of this hand there are, according to Jahn, who never saw it, but copied Montfaucon, a lyre, pincers, cymbals, Phrygian flute, knife, and a phallus. The two caps here

HORNS OF HONOR

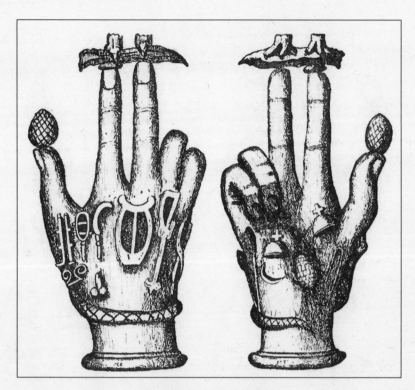

Figs. 110, 111. British Museum.

represented are manifestly the same as the single one on Fig. 107, which Meyer calls a bell. We see that there are two Phrygian flutes as in other examples, and that the so-called knife is the well-known pruning-hook, symbol of both Bacchus and Priapus. There is also the *sistrum*, [88] sacred to Isis, and a large object, possibly meant for a *caduceus*, but not to be identified with certainty. It has been suggested that this may be the *mystica vannus Iacchi* of Virgil, an ancient winnowing implement borne often in the processions celebrated in honour of Bacchus and Ceres: or at least it may be the old winnowing shovel, symbolic of those divinities, who were proper guardians of agriculture and rural life. The special features to be noted in this

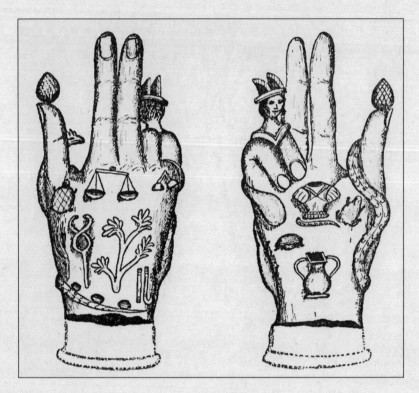

Figs. 112, 113. Gori.

unique hand are the crescent, the lyre, the tongs of Vulcan, and the phallus. Upon these we shall have much to say in our next chapter.

Figs. 112–113 are from Gori, cited by Jahn (*e*), but it does not appear where the hand was found, nor where it is at present. Gori writes upon this, that it is undoubtedly sacred to Mercury, and that the right hand was dedicated to him whenever his image appears upon it. He goes on to repeat the old story about these hands being *ex votos*, but his only evidence relates to the one bearing the inscription by Cecropius, and, according to him, it was this hand which Cecropius dedicated! He enumerates a number of articles offered to the gods, and also many objects sacred to them severally. He says the eyes, tongue, teeth, breast, etc., represented the parts healed, and that they were made of gold, silver, ivory, precious stones, crystal, and even of bronze; still others of wax, wood and clay (terra-cotta). All this is precisely true of the objects hung up in his time, and in the churches of to-day, but there is not a scrap of evidence that these pantheistic hands were ever *ex votos*, in the sense of being so devoted in temples, etc. Gori remarks on the identity of gesture in every one of them, and that the thumb, index, and middle fingers being raised while the others are closed, is because these were considered more apt at numeration; but he says he cannot account for the closing of the *medicus* and *minimus*. At the same time he refers to Numa having dedicated this sign to denote 300 on the right hand and 65 on the left. The cuirass of Mars and the three little pots are new features; so is the second tortoise on the palm near the *cantharus*. Its position, no less than its curious foreshortening, is remarkable. One little pot similar to these is upon the Payne Knight hand (Fig. 90), and we would point out, regarding this difference in the numbers of the same objects, that on one hand (Fig. 111) we have two caps, and in another (Fig. 107), one of the self-same kind; so we have two frogs, and four cakes, against one and three in other hands.

Figs. 114–115 (page 194) are from Montfaucon (Bonanni Coll.), ii. pi. 137. This hand was found in 1708 on the Isola Farnese in Rome, and used to be in the museum of the Collegio Romano, now merged in the Kirscherian, but it has disappeared. It is (*d*) in Jahn's list, who simply copied Bonanni, from *Antichita di Ercolano*, vol. i. p. 5.

The termination of the thumb in the head of Serapis is very remarkable, and together with the ram's head, of course denotes the

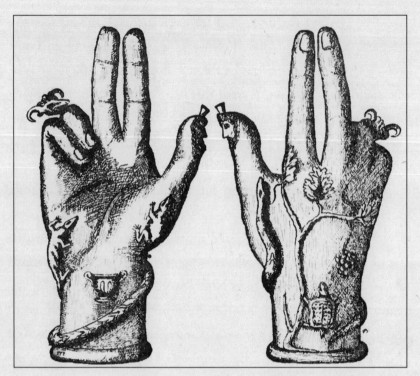

Figs. 114, 115. Isola Farnese, Montfaucon.

dedication of the hand to him and to Mercury as the principal deities. Again we find the *cantharus* of Bacchus on the front, and a unique example of a vine bearing fruit on the back of the hand, which go to prove that he was the other principal god worshipped thereby. This is an interesting specimen showing nearly the same variety in the combination of attributes, compared with other hands, as we find to-day in the modern pantheistic cimaruta.

Figs. 116–117 are from *Dissertazioni della Pia Accademia di Archaeologia* (Roma, 1836, vol. vii. p. 427), cited as (*i*) in Jahn's list. It was found at Valeria in Cagli about 1833. Where the hand is at present is unknown. Wanting the eagle, it is said to be of the exact size of the original drawing, which is just six inches high. In

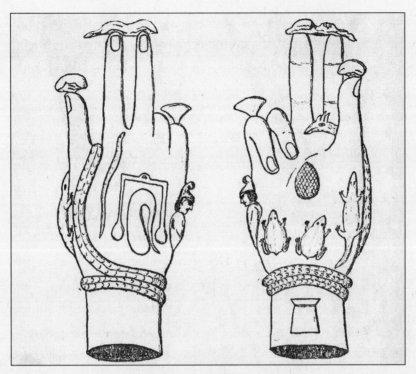

Figs. 116, 117. Valeria in Cagli.

many respects it is peculiar, for while the pine-cone in the centre of the palm seems perhaps to denote Sabazius, but more probably Cybele, the figure in the Phrygian cap not being bearded is very likely intended for Atys, who was worshipped along with her. It has been suggested by Mr. Marindin that this head may be that of Mithras, who was usually represented as a youth in a Phrygian cap.[89] On the tips of the fingers are the undoubted symbols of Jupiter in the thunderbolt, and in the eagle, which once stood upon it. The proximity of the two frogs points to the licentious orgies connected with the cult of Cybele; or possibly to the Sabazia.

Within the balance, on the back, is an object similar in shape to that seen on *post* Fig. 127, which seems to the present writer to be the bag or purse of Mercury, a less common symbol than the *caduceus* or the tortoise; but Jahn calls this object *ein Muschel* (uterus), sacred to Juno Lucina. We should venture to take exception to Jahn's opinion on the ground that several undoubted *uteri*, which have been true *ex votos*, are to be seen in terra-cotta in the museums of Naples, Paris, and Oxford (Ashmolean); but there is nothing in their general shape at all corresponding with the two symbols upon the hands now

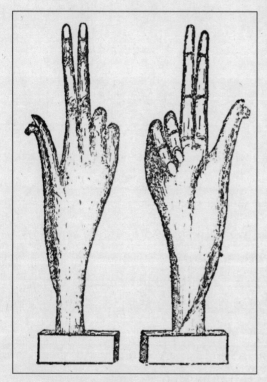

being considered. The objects upon the pollex and minimus are obscure, and it is doubtful whether the article on the wrist is intended for a vase or *ambos* (anvil). The modelling and finish are apparently poor, while inasmuch as the original is no longer to be seen in any public museum, we are unable to supply a sketch from the original.

Figs. 118–119 are taken from a hand in the Kirscherian Museum at Rome now first published. It is a small, ill-moulded hand, extremely

Figs. 118, 119. Kirscherian.

long and thin, but evidently of the same character as the rest, and dedicated solely to Æsculapius. There is a similar one in the Naples Museum (No. 19), found at Herculaneum, having only a single serpent upon it, but of this we omitted to make a sketch. We find,

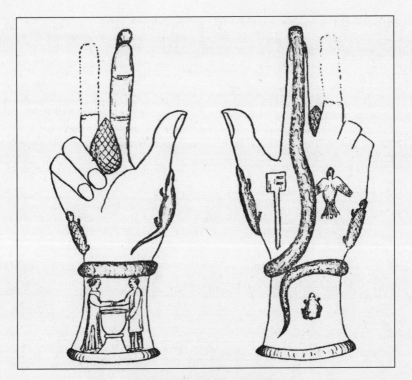

Figs. 120, 121. Leyden, Jahn (*m*).

however, that every one of these hands, so far as we know at present, has one or more serpents upon it, even when there is no other symbol.

Figs. 120–121 depict a very remarkable specimen, now in the museum at Leyden, of which no drawing has hitherto been published.[90] It has been referred to by Herr Meyer (*ante*, p. 240) and by Jahn, who merely cites it in his list as (*m*); but they fail to note several peculiarities. The serpent climbing to the top of the index is a new and unique feature. The pine-cone in the place of honour, like Fig. 117, points to Cybele. The strange object like a spade cannot be identified nor its mystery solved, though a friend has suggested that it may be a *sistrum*. The bird is also seen for the first time in this position; it is probably meant for a dove, and in that case is identical with the bird perched on the thumb (Fig. 106).

Of course the chief interest in this example lies in the man and woman joining hands over a large vase or altar, and it is submitted with some confidence that the whole hand is thereby interpreted. It must surely be intended as the special household appeal for protection and help, by a newly-wedded pair, to the gods whose symbols are embossed thereon.

Figs. 122–123 are from another hand in the museum at Zurich. It was found at Sion, in Canton Valais, and although when first seen the writer believed it to be unpublished, he has since seen a lithograph of this hand in *Mittheilungen der Antiquarischen Gesellschaft,* Zurich, 1861 (Band xiii. Abth. 2, heft 4), but no light is thrown

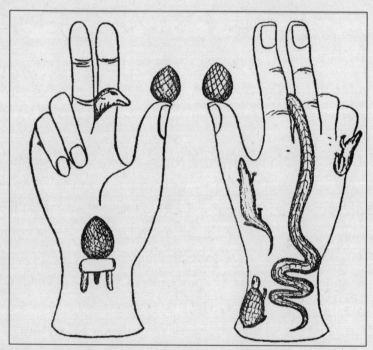

Figs. 122, 123. Zurich, found at Sion, Valais.

upon it in the text. The cone upon the tripod is the feature in this hand, occupying the place of honour on the palm, and showing by the two cones that the whole is probably an invocation to Cybele. We have already described (p. 183) a hand in the Louvre bearing three pine-cones. The serpent peeping out between the first and second fingers is a new position.

Figs. 124–125 represent the famous hand formerly in Lord Londesborough's collection, bearing the Greek inscription so much discussed by Jahn and others. It is now to be seen in the British Museum, and has not hitherto been published. It will be found to be rather an insignificant example, and, except for the inscription here repeated, not of special interest. This latter is indistinct, and is here given upon Jahn's authority—he cites this hand as *n* in his list, and

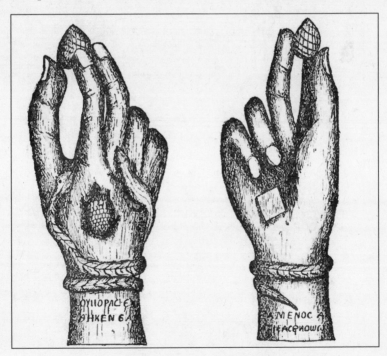

Figs. 124, 125. British Museum.

THE *MANO PANTEA*, OR SYMBOLIC HAND 199

renders the words into modern Greek letters as Ζουπορας ευξαμευος αυεθηκευ Σαβαζιφ. This is of course one of the dedications so much relied upon to prove these hands to be *ex votos*. There is, however, no evidence that the inscription was not added at some time long subsequent to the casting of the hand. It is, we submit, one of the few special exceptions of express dedication which show that these hands were not primarily, nor generally intended for *ex votos*. Examples so accessible as those in the British Museum can be well left to explain themselves to any who desire to study them further.

Figs. 126–127 are from another hand in the British Museum, belonging to the class with which we are dealing, and chiefly remarkable as the only one of the series without a serpent, unless the

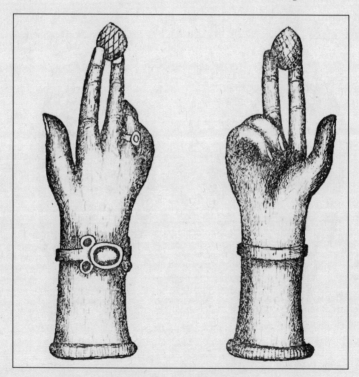

Figs. 126, 127. British Museum.

HORNS OF HONOR

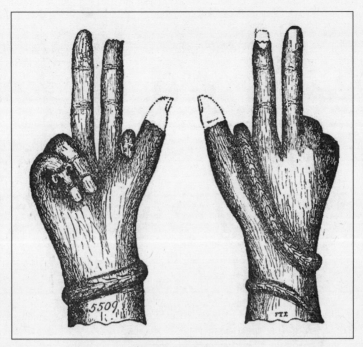

Figs. 128, 129. Naples.

bracelet is intended to take the place of it. This is a recent acquisition, and hitherto unpublished.

Figs. 128–129 are from a hand in the Naples Museum, No. 5509, hitherto unnoted and unpublished, found recently at Pompeii. The only objects upon it are of the usual type, and in positions found on other examples. Its chief interest lies in the place where it was discovered, thus fixing approximately the date of all these hands.

Figs. 130–131 (page 202) are from the original in the Museum at Cortona, never before published. It is a specimen of exceeding interest, and is the one which first drew the present writer's attention many years ago to these remarkable remains of ancient Roman life, though at that time he omitted to take a sketch of it. The annexed

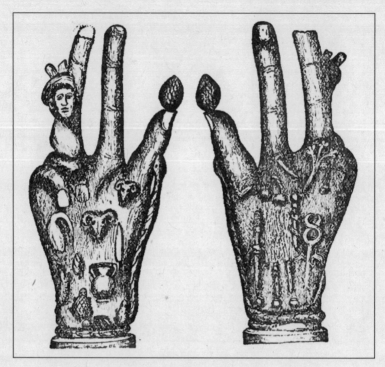

Figs. 130, 131. Cortona.

illustration is drawn from photographs taken specially for the writer. Most of the objects upon it are familiar, and have been already discussed. The purse-like, long-necked bag is similar to that on Fig.

Fig. 132. Naples.

116, and being placed under Mercury seems to show the hand to be dedicated to him. The small tripod at the wrist is without offering upon it. The three small pots or vases have been noted on other hands, Figs. 91, 109, but cannot be explained. Mercury is evidently the protagonist, for besides his bust, we have two rams' heads, the purse, *caduceus* and crocodile.

Fig. 132 is a small example from the original in the Naples Museum, No. 5461. It is three inches high, and has only a pine-cone for Cybele and a serpent on it. From the unfailing appearance of the serpent, we cannot but conclude that whatever gods the Romans worshipped besides, Æsculapius was never omitted; that health was the one thing they never forgot to pray for.

Over and above all the examples which the present writer has been able to bring together, it is well known that there are very many others existing that he has had no opportunity of examining, or of which no drawings have been published. Dr. Becker, in *Die Heddernheimer Votivhand* (Frankfurt, 1861), cites a considerable number of hands, presumably of this kind, including several of those here dealt with; indeed he numbers thirty in all, but as they are but imperfect descriptions, without plates or sketches, it is impossible to form any accurate conclusion as to whether they all belong to the distinct class with which we have been dealing. The student is directed to the brochure itself, and particularly so because the self-same hand, which gives the title to the paper, and is illustrated by a drawing nine inches high, said to be *naturliche grosse*, is not a *mano pantea* at all, but a plain open hand, already sufficiently discussed.

One very remarkable fact is established by the bringing together of so many examples; there is no known duplicate, nor are any two so precisely similar that it would have been possible to produce them from the same mould. In the one or two cases where the general shape or distribution of the symbols resembles that of another example, there is either a marked difference in the size of the hands themselves, or the several symbols upon them bear distinct individuality, either in size or modelling, or in both.

From this we gather that it must have been customary for every individual who possessed one to have it specially made for himself, different in some detail from every other. We are supported in this opinion by finding the highly composite amulets made for sale to-day in conservative modern Naples, to be all differing in some particular or other. We have never seen two *cimarute* nor two *sirene* precisely alike.

The large number of these remarkable hands, which are known still to exist, is of itself a very important fact, and proves decisively that they must once have been exceedingly common in Roman households. It may well be maintained that no one speciality of Roman life is represented by so large a number of the same object, manifestly intended for religious use, as the *mano pantea*. We infer from this fact that it must have been of such daily use, and so extremely common, as to have escaped all record. So far as we know, there is no reference to these hands in any classical or even later writer until quite modern times—indeed the very earliest mention of any one of them is no older than the seventeenth century; nor so far as we can ascertain is there any remaining tradition in Italy or elsewhere which can in any way throw light upon them. We are thus left to form an opinion as to their use, solely upon such evidence as may be provided by a study of the hands themselves, and by the places and circumstances in which they have been found. Only one out of all that have been unearthed has been discovered in or near any temple. Even that one, said to have been found in the ruins of the temple of Jupiter Penninus on Mount St. Bernard, may have well belonged to the household effects of those who served the temple in that solitary spot. There is nothing to identify it except De Loges' description. He says it was cast in a mould: that the two last fingers were closed on the palm; on the tip of the thumb was an excrescence like a pine-cone. A crested (*huppé*) serpent was entwined between the index and *annulaire*. It seemed to bite into the hand. In front on the wrist was a *bonnet pontifical*; on the back of the hand were a frog and a lizard.

This does not correspond with any one of the hands here illustrated, and if still in existence its present resting place is unknown. It may be remarked that the *bonnet pontifical* must have been a repetition of the cap on Figs. 107–111, which we know to symbolise one or both of the Dioscuri,[91] and his description only shows how careless and slovenly have been the few writers who have noted the figures embossed on these important remains of pagan Rome. No doubt, however, we have here a description by De Loges of a distinct and undoubted *mano pantea* no longer accessible, yet differing from any known example.

Comparing the many specimens bearing the recumbent woman and child, with the Leyden hand (Fig. 120) bearing the man and woman together, we submit with all confidence that the latter is the missing link, disposing of the very broken chain by which they have been dubbed *ex votos*, *i.e.*, thank offerings in acknowledgment for favours received. They have all been found, with one exception, in or about domestic buildings, and we maintain therefore that they were accessories of home life; that being obviously religious they were the household protectors, like the teraphin of the Israelites,[92] and that they were veritable *penates*, representing powerful beings in whom their possessors believed; and that these hands held in Roman families the same place as statuettes of Madonna or of saints do in Italian families to-day.

Is there anything among all the mountains of modern literature, that if preserved would hand down to posterity a thousand or fifteen hundred years hence, any description of the appearance, material, use or cult of the little images to be seen to-day in the windows of so-called religious depositories, whether in Rome, Paris, or London? Where do we read any mention, likely to inform posterity, of the thousands of little bronze copies of St. Peter of the Vatican? Will they in the year 3500 leave more remains than we find now of the *mano pantea*? How much less likely then is it that we should now be able to find any mention of these ancient objects of reverence!

We believe and hope to prove in our next chapter that these symbol-bearing hands were but a development of something much older still, and a connecting link which has helped to hand down to these latter days the very ancient idea that safety is found not only in the protection of one powerful being, but is made more certain by addition and accumulation of a number of their names or symbols into one composite whole, such for example as we find in the dedication of guilds, hospitals, abbeys, or churches, to St. Mary and St. Peter, to SS. Paul and Barnabas, to St. Michael and All Angels, or to All Saints.

Inasmuch as several of the examples here cited have been unearthed in obscure cases in great museums or in small local ones, it is sincerely hoped that all who are interested in the subject will take note of any other specimens of these very remarkable hands that may come in their way, in order that still more data may be brought together for the elucidation of their true meaning and use. Further, it is to be hoped that classical mythologists will be induced by the considerable materials herein placed at their disposal, to study more closely and with greater knowledge the exact and specific symbols embossed on these hands, so that their precise significance, as well as their historical and traditional connection with the deities they undoubtedly represent, may be completely and accurately understood.

CHAPTER V.

DISCHI SACRI

I N DEALING WITH THIS subject after that of the *mano pantea* we must face the charge of inconsistency, or of putting the cart before the horse. Our inquiries and our methods are perforce purely inductive, and depend solely upon the collection of facts. We have no desire, as we have no opportunity, to be consistent. Our evidence must speak for itself, and perhaps like testimony of other kinds is often conflicting; our object is merely to state what is true and to leave experts to explain and to harmonise that which appears contradictory.

It therefore comes naturally and not designedly that we should have to trace backwards towards their beginnings the curious hands with which we have been dealing, rather than to take the earlier objects we have now to consider. The title here adopted is, like that of the previous chapter, purely local. It is that given on the spot to a large number of fragments in terra-cotta, lately discovered in the Italian Government excavations at Taranto. Those with which we are now concerned are all flat discs or plaques, mostly circular in shape, from half to three-quarters of an inch in thickness, and although nearly all are broken, it is easy to see that in their original and perfect state they were of various dimensions, ranging from four to eighteen or twenty inches in diameter.

The largest of these in the writer's possession are not covered with small and distinct objects like those here shown, but have each a gorgon's head of the early, grinning, split-tongued type as a centre, round which in concentric circles run well-known Greek patterns, such as, especially, the *meander* or key-pattern, the egg and dart, and the *anthemion*. These are described as the "chief characteristics of the geometrical style" of the middle Greek period, known now as "Dipylon" from the great finds in the cemetery outside that gate at Athens, where so many of those typical ornaments have been brought to light.

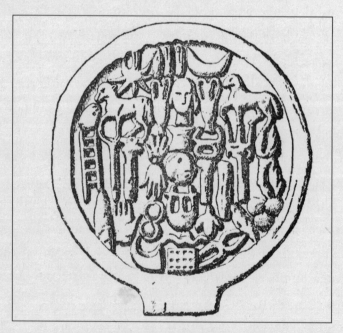

Fig. 133. Terra-cotta Disc in the British Museum.

Upon all the discs are a variety of objects which, from our previous study of the pantheistic hands, we recognise at once as symbolic. Most of those recently found are evidently moulds, that is, the symbols upon them are sunk, and are intended to produce a raised impression upon whatever material is applied to them. On the other hand, a few of the Tarentine find are in themselves *camei, i.e.* finished positives, having the objects upon them *in relievo*.

Previous to the discoveries of the last twenty years, two only of these remarkable discs were known, and upon those two alone has been mainly founded all that has hitherto been written about them, which amounts to very little. The best-known specimen is the single one in the British Museum, presented by the late Sir William Temple, and said to have been found at Pozzuoli. Fig. 133 is a representation of this disc, about which the first notice appears in Jahn's treatise, who speaks of it as a curious monument and a distinct amulet. It is quite evident, however, that he had never seen the object itself, but only a drawing which he copies. (*Op. cit.*, tav. v. 3.)

In his note Jahn says that his illustration is one-third of the size of the original, whereas his drawing is 3¾ in. by 4½ in., while the original is exactly 4⅝ in. by 5 in. No observer would be so careless as to estimate the disc in the British Museum as measuring 11¼ in. by 13½ in., therefore it is clear he only wrote at second hand.

The second well-known example is in the Naples Museum, of which Fig. 134 (page 212) is a fairly correct sketch. This is nearly the same size as the Temple disc, being 4¼ in. by 5½ in., the greater length being accounted for by the longer projection or foot. It was found at Pompeii, and was of course well known to Minervini, the editor of *Bullettino Archeologico Napolitano*, No. 120, 1857, *an. v.*

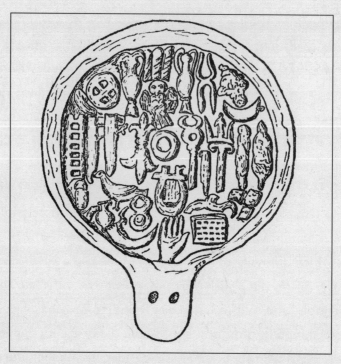

Fig. 134. Terra-cotta Disc in the Museo Nazionale, Naples, No. 5466.

tav. vi., in which he gives a plate and full description. In his article on it he refers to Jahn's account of that in the British Museum (Fig. 133), and criticises some of Jahn's identifications of the several symbols. He implies, by speaking of these *due notabili monumenti*, that there were no others in existence—in any case he knew of no more.

In the *Gazette Archéologique*, 1883, p. 7, is a plate of another of these plaques now in the Louvre, of which Fig. 135 is a copy. The size is not given, and we have not yet seen the original, but presume it to measure about the same as the other two previously noted. Heydemann, who had previously seen the articles in the *Bullettino Archeologico Napolitano*, 1857, by Heuzey and Minervini, upon the Naples disc (Fig. 134), writes that he neither agrees with Heuzey

Fig. 135. *Gazette Archéologique*, Louvre.

that the object of these "moulds" was to impress the objects on them upon sacrificial cakes; nor with François Lenormant (who writes in the same volume), that they served for the making of lamps. He gives his own opinion, to which we refer later, and with which we cordially agree. He confesses that he is unable to identify many of the symbols.

In the same volume of the *Gazette* is an article by Lenormant, being a report of an archaeological expedition to Southern Italy on behalf of the French Government. He describes a fragment of one of these "moulds" which he discovered at Metaponto, gives a drawing of it (Fig. 136 on page 214), and says it is larger in size than either of those he has seen before, but he does not say what has become of it.

Besides these, Heydemann refers to another of these "moulds" as being at Berlin, but we have had no opportunity of seeing it or of obtaining a sketch; we therefore assume that both these examples are correctly described as *moules*; *i.e.,* having the symbols sunk, not embossed.

Here the matter rested, until Mr. Arthur J. Evans obtained another (Fig. 137), now in the Ashmolean Museum at Oxford, together with two fragments obtained at the same time, of which one has a gorgon's head in the centre. In 1886 Mr. Evans wrote an important article, entitled "Recent Discoveries of Tarentine Terra-Cottas," in which he deals with those now in the Ashmolean. The heading of the section about these discs is "Moulds for Sacred Cakes,"

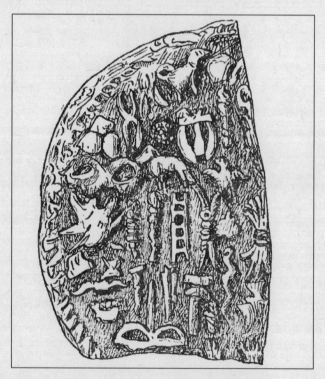

Fig. 136. *Gazette Archéologique*, 1883, p. 79.

and though it is true that the examples at Oxford are moulds, *i.e.*, *intagliati*, he assumes that all others known are of the same kind, and he follows Heuzey and Minervini in the supposition that as moulds they were intended to make raised impressions on the sacred cakes offered to the gods. Further, he truly remarks that the resemblance of the other two described by Jahn and Minervini to the specimens he had brought from Tarentum leads to the fair presumption that all alike had come originally from the same place. In this we may agree, but it is a singular example of careless observation that both Heuzey and Minervini, who had the object itself under their own eyes, should have described it as a mould, and so have imagined a use for it as such, when all the time both it and the disc at the British Museum

Fig. 137. Terra-cotta Disc in the Ashmolean Museum, Oxford.

DISCHI SACRI

were manifestly nothing of the kind, for both discs are cameos and not moulds—they are actually finished casts taken from some other moulds, such as those which Mr. Evans has at Oxford. It was not until after he had obtained facsimiles, and carefully re-examined the discs in London and Naples, that the present writer discovered that he had been mistaken in assuming the correctness of other writers. He has consequently to withdraw his statement on p. 376 of *The Evil Eye*, and to affirm, on the contrary, that both the discs known to Jahn, Heuzey, and Minervini are not moulds but reliefs. This fact entirely upsets and changes all that has hitherto been written about them, notwithstanding the remarks of Heydemann and Lenormant. It is the inaccuracy of Heuzey and Minervini that is responsible for all the sacred cake theory. Jahn does not hazard an opinion as to the purpose for which these terra-cotta plaques were intended, he probably never saw either of them; but he readily perceived that they were pantheistic objects, and he goes into details as to the symbols upon them, and as to the deities whom they were intended to represent.

In *Walpole's Memoirs*, p. 452, a plaque of this kind is mentioned, but the account is too vague to show whether he refers to a copy of that in the British Museum, or to that now said to be in Berlin, or to some other. It is possible he may have seen one of those subsequently obtained by Mr. Evans.

Up to 1896 the examples referred to above were the only ones known, and only by the present writer had even so many as three of these been brought together for comparison and study. In that year, however, being at Taranto, he saw that there had been a great find of these remarkable discs—a few perfect, but for the most part in fragments. The result was that in February, 1898, he was able to exhibit to the Society of Antiquaries no less than fifty-four out of his sixty-four casts, and facsimiles of that number of different, entire or parts of, *dischi sacri*, no two of which are alike; and here we may recall attention to the same remarkable fact of individuality regarding the pantheistic hands treated in the last chapter—a fact which cannot but be of great significance.

The bulk of the new specimens found at Taranto are moulds, but two or three are not; they are reliefs like the discs in London and Naples, and consequently the plaster casts in the writer's collection are, with those exceptions, in similar relief to that at the British Museum, which of course is an original.

The writer's specimens are of all sizes, from the finished disc of four inches to fragments of eighteen inches in diameter. These larger ones (2) have each a gorgon's head of the early split-tongued type in the centre.

The writer hoped that by exhibiting these strange remains of antiquity to the world of science at the British Association and the Society of Antiquaries, together with the publication of his notes in their *Proceedings*, much light would be thrown upon the interesting questions of their use and history. The great number of fragments, each representing a different and distinct plaque, being found in the same place, seems to point to the fragments as patterns rather than broken pieces—indeed many show no signs of fracture, though evidently only segments or portions of the entire article; and one cannot but believe that a manufacturer's stock of patterns must have been lighted on.

In any case their number proves them to have been in common demand, at least in that part of Magna Graecia where they were found in bulk. That three or four specimens only have been found in other parts of Italy, and nowhere else, proves nothing. The material being fragile, and the objects of no artistic value, would fully account for their disappearance.

We must then assume that whatever else they were, they were primarily household effects. They certainly were crude and common even in their day, pronounced by experts to have been not later than 300 BC, probably about the time of the Greco-Roman transition. We know that the makers of these things were capable of much better things, for among this very find were found finely moulded heads and other works, proving them to be no mean artists. Many of these heads, too, are not mere broken pieces of statues, but finished models, as though they also were intended for patterns. Of these latter the writer possesses many remarkable specimens, showing distinctly the transition from the early Greek to the Greco-Roman and Roman types.

On careful comparison of all these different discs, it is found that notwithstanding their individuality and diversity of treatment, there is a very obvious regularity and system, both in the position and combination of the many figures embossed upon them. Not only do we find the same object, say the trident or the *caduceus*, repeated over and over again on different specimens, but they generally are placed near each other, frequently in line, with some other object between. The constant appearance, moreover, of the *caduceus* upon these discs cannot but recall the same frequent appearance of that symbol upon the *mano pantea*. Other symbols, like the lyre, the dove, the three cakes, the wheel-cross, found alike upon the hands and discs, cannot be accidental, and we must admit that whatever was intended or typified by the objects upon the hands, had surely an earlier existence upon the discs. Many of the symbols on the latter have no place upon the hands, but time would account for changes of fashion in that respect, just as it would doubtless for the total disappearance of the fragile discs themselves; while greater riches, and the consequent increase in the use of bronze, would cause the more durable form of the metal hand to take the place of terra-cotta as the foundation on which to emboss the sacred symbols. Besides all this, other reasons of a religious nature probably tended to supersede the fragile disc by the uplifted hand.

Sacred we certainly hold all the symbols to be, whether in bronze or terra-cotta. It will not fail to be noticed, however, that the hand itself, though open, appears on no less than seven out of the eleven illustrations here given; moreover, these seven specimens were selected as a mere sample of the whole, and by no means because they are even the best examples or because they have these hands, much less to support any theory whatever, for the open hand appears on a large proportion of the whole. It will be noted that the discs are of two distinct kinds as regards arrangement of symbols. One kind, as in Figs. 133, 138, 139, has them in lines, so far as a circular limit permits, while the other has them grouped roughly, like the spokes of a wheel, as in Figs. 135, 137, 145. The former kind is much the more frequent.

Figs. 133, 134 are, at first sight, strikingly alike, and there are many more which, seen apart and not measured or closely examined, would probably be called duplicates. So it is with the hands—bring them together and the difference becomes immediately evident. Again, symbols on some of the discs are very indistinct and difficult to identify, whereas what is obscure on one is often plain on another;

so that by comparing them together one specimen constantly makes clear what is doubtful on others. For example, in Fig. 130 the ladder is obvious enough, but the next two objects in line with it, upon which a sheep (? ram) is standing, are indescribable; but on turning to Fig. 134 we see that nearly the entire row is identical, and there it is quite plain that the two figures doubtful on the former are a torch and a scabbard: both these symbols are to be found on the bronze hands.

Fig. 138 is a most valuable fragment of the linear type, containing a large number of symbols, some of which (*e.g.*, two wheel-crosses, two plain crosses, two scabbards) seem to be duplicated, another feature to be remarked on one or two of the hands as well

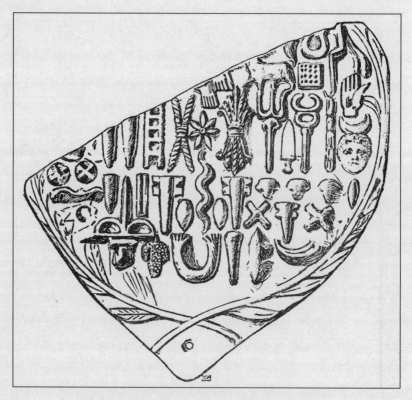

Fig. 138. Terra-cotta Disc found at Taranto (1/2 linear).

HORNS OF HONOR

as on these plaques. The grapes also are seen on the hands. We note, however, that on the discs only two or three out of the entire number have a serpent, of which this is one, and the lizard is entirely absent. From this we infer that the influence of Egypt became persistent at a period later than these *dischi sacri*, but earlier than the *mano pantea*. The head of Diana is obvious enough on this and another, while the foliated border in low relief, we submit once more, completely disposes of the sacred-cake theory.

There are, of course, many symbols which cannot be identified. Of these, one is the kind of St. Andrew's cross next to the ladder, appearing also on the next illustration, and on many other discs. Another is the square object with a number of holes in line; this is a very frequent one, and occurs in no less than seven of our few illustrations, besides on many more of those in the writer's collection. The curved thing in five of the foregoing figures, near the bottom, might be intended for a cornucopia, but it looks like an exaggerated tiger's tooth. It is a strange commentary, moreover, that the writer possesses several tiger's teeth in metal, coral, and other material, mounted and sold to be worn as modern charms against the evil eye; but the fact is that these are really intended for a dolphin, as will be seen on careful examination of all the originals. The two hands, joined by a kind of half-circle, are strikingly like the Egyptian hieroglyph *Ka*. It will be noticed that there are also no less than three scabbards for Ares (Mars) and two wheel-crosses, besides two other Greek crosses, and the seven-rayed sun in the centre.

Fig. 139 is another interesting segment, very like the last, but how different! Although drawn to the same scale as the previous one, it has many less symbols upon it, for the reason that each separate one is of

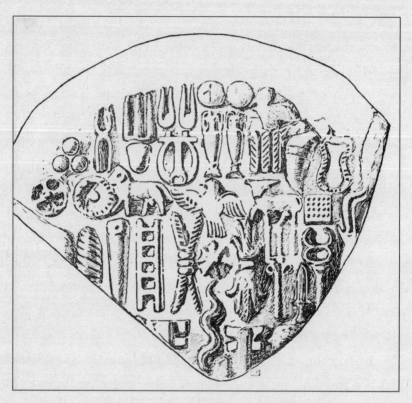

Fig. 139. Terra-cotta Disc found at Taranto (1/2 linear).

a much larger size. It will be noticed that the arrangement is identical, but on the centre line there is no room in this latter beyond the *caduceus* (this is not so distinctly shown on the drawing as it appears in the original), consequently the club of Hercules, Diana's head and the hand are left out. Nevertheless this plaque is complete on the top where Fig. 138 is deficient, so that we are in a way able to complete the latter. In both, one of the rams stands on the trident, a position occupied also in Fig. 133, but here the other ram is above the ladder.

Fig. 140 is another bordered example, having comparatively few, though well-defined, symbols. The two sheep are in quite a new position. The object above the bird is the *sistrum* of Isis, found on

Fig. 140. Terra-cotta Disc found at Taranto (1/2 linear).

many other of the discs. The kind of bench above the *sistrum*, on which are the two *amphorae*, is found, on two or three others, and is quite a new feature. There is no doubt as to its meaning, confirmed certainly by the two vases above it. The vases, and the object on which they stand, are alternative symbols of the Dioscuri, who were much worshipped among the Greeks, and whose symbols appear upon the hands (round cap with cross or star on the top).

According to Roscher,[93] two vertical beams, with two others bound across them, was the most ancient symbol of the deities known to the Romans as Castor and Pollux. This same symbol is still the astronomical sign of Gemini.

The next symbol in antiquity was, according to the same authority, two *amphorae*, with or without serpents upon them.

No less than ten different symbols of these deities, including the round, star-crowned hats, are enumerated by Roscher.

We find, too, that the Dioscuri were worshipped as gods of the sea, hence we should expect to find them held in such great reverence at Tarentum as to lead to a doubling of their symbols.

The knotted rope next to the central wheel-cross, which appears on several other discs, cannot be identified.

The tongs of Vulcan (Hephaistos) appear on every one of the foregoing discs, and on one of the hands. The remarkable feature of this and one other of the plaques is the cross *botonée* in the centre. Many students of modern heraldry will be surprised to see this device so early as 300 BC, and in such company! Long before the Crusades, however, yet many centuries later than our plaques, this same device was the badge of the Roman Legion of the West—called Constantia.

Fig. 141 is a small plaque with few but very large and distinct symbols upon it. Those at the top on either side of the hand appear in several, but we must leave others to explain them. The modern astronomical sign for the "ascending node" is like this, but it does not seem to denote any planet or constellation. In this the ladder is very prominent, and as an emblem in these discs is almost as frequent as is the serpent on the hand, but it is by no means easy to determine which of the deities is intended to be represented by it. Jahn, in writing upon it, is very doubtful as to its signification, and finishes with something like a guess that it is the symbol of Aphrodite. Minervini, on the other hand, disagrees with Jahn, talks of the

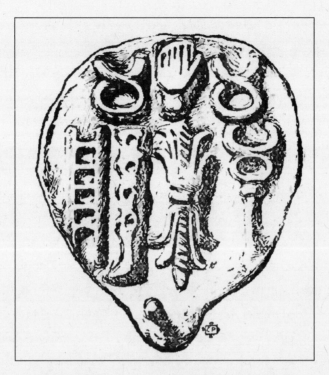

Fig. 141. Terra-cotta Disc found at Taranto (1/2 linear).

pretesa scaletta, and maintains that it is the web of a loom (*arnese da tessere*) and is a symbol of Ceres. Had he seen all the specimens we could show him, he and Millingen, whom he quotes, would both admit that all this is mere nonsense. The object is an undoubted ladder; moreover very many of the ancient symbols found on these ancient discs have survived as modern charms against the "evil eye." Of those on these very discs the writer has in his own collection two ladders, a lyre, two *canthari*, pincers of Vulcan, *caduceus*, tiger's teeth, hands, wheel (of fortune), sun, crescent, owl, dove, cock, bunch of grapes, knife, sheep in bone, precisely like those on Fig. 133 (the latter well worn), pruning-hook of Priapus, whip of Osiris, etc. There is, therefore, not the shadow of a doubt as to the object so often repeated being a ladder, and the only difficulty is to explain satisfactorily its significance.

Fortuna, Bona Dea, Tyche was one of the most favourite goddesses of the ancients. She or her symbols appear constantly. On the lamp we show later (Fig. 147) she is the central figure, bearing a cornucopia, one of her special symbols; the many wheels too, or wheel-crosses, upon the discs, especially on Figs. 138, 139, although properly sun signs, may possibly be intended for her wheel, still considered in these latter days as the emblem of her revolving favours. Fortune's wheel, however, is but the sign of one of her aspects—the changeable, unexpected, fortuitous; while the cornucopia signifies the abundant plenty she has brought to, or is hoped for by her suppliant. A third aspect is, we believe, symbolised by the ladder, that of the patient, climbing, striving, persistent suitor, who sues her by his own efforts and means to scale her heights; to win by patient perseverance the favours she was believed to bestow. Hence "the ladder of fortune" is no less one of her symbols than her wheel. This will be made evident by a study of two or three facts.

In the *Book of the Dead* we find much about the ladder. We read that the ancient Egyptians believed one part of a man only could mount to heaven, and that by means of a ladder. "In the pyramid of Pepi I." we read: "Hail to thee, O Ladder of God, hail to thee, O Ladder of Set. Stand up, O Ladder of God, stand up, O Ladder of Set, stand up, O Ladder of Horus, whereon Osiris went forth to Heaven."

By this we see that the notion of a connection between earth and heaven by a ladder was quite familiar to the Egyptians, and doubtless to the whole Eastern world. Hence we may fairly assume that Jacob's dream was not the unaided first product of his brain, but that it was a result, and well accorded with the notions and beliefs of the age in which he lived, influenced, as we know they were, by the close connection of the patriarchs with Egypt. Allowing for the confusions in mythology, on which we have dwelt fully here and elsewhere, the ladder of Horus, Set, Osiris, and Jacob may well have become that of Tyche, the Fortune of the Greeks, and later of the Romans.

Next, the discs on which the ladder we are discussing is found, are distinctly Greco-Roman of early date (fourth century BC). They were found in Apulia, one of the earliest settled parts of Magna Graecia, and there, if anywhere, we might expect to find the ladder, used as a symbol upon other objects. We are not disappointed. In the British Museum are many ancient Greek vases from Apulia, and we are told that we must look to vases not only for the illustration of passages familiar to us in ancient literature, but also for the preservation of much that would otherwise be lost "relating to manners and social

life." On several of these vases is to be found a ladder, sometimes held in the hand and sometimes suspended or standing alone, but in every case where it appears there is indication of a love scene. Either Aphrodite, Adonis, Eros, or Hermes are in close contact with it.

Fig 142. Apulian Vase, 308, British Museum.

Fig. 142 represents a standing female, believed to be Tyche, holding out a ladder, sketched from No. 308 vase. On 331 is a female sitting, but holding a ladder in her right hand, and in her left an open box held at arm's length in the opposite direction. It is here suggested this is no other than Pandora, and that while with one hand she holds out the symbol of successful love, she seems to be holding out behind her the open box symbolic of all the evils and misfortunes accompanying licentious passion. No. 272 has the ladder as a separate symbol. Vase No. 414 has a winged Eros holding out a ladder of fifteen rounds in his right hand.

Fig. 143. Apulian Vase, 373.

Fig. 143 is from another of these (No. 373) fine vases, showing Eros holding the *crux ansata*, with a ladder at his feet. Several of these vases, moreover, represent some of the manual gestures with which we have been dealing, as well as the objects now under consideration. On 331 is a sitting female, making the sign of the *mano cornuta*, upwards, towards a winged Eros. On 308, another sitting figure is making the sign of the *mano pantea* with her right hand, while holding a fish in the left (a modern charm). Facing her is another female holding up a very perfect umbrella! On 332 is Mercury, leaning on a fountain making the sign of the *mano pantea*, and in his left hand holding the *caduceus*.

On No. 160 are Castor and Pollux, both wearing the conical caps shown on the hand (Fig. 111). One is making the sign of *mano pantea* with the right hand, while his left wrist is grasped by his companion. We give these particulars here because they are so accessible and easily verified by all interested.

Much to the surprise of the writer, in all cases the ladder on these vases is described in the Museum Catalogue as an Apulian *sistrum*, but no authority is vouchsafed, and we submit, with much deference, that none is to be found. On the other hand there are several writers who doubt not that these are veritable ladders. Heydemann, no mean authority, gives two interpretations of the ladder—one, that it was symbolic; the other, the obvious one, that it was a domestic implement. He believes the ladders upon Apulian vases to be the symbol of Fortuna. On the other hand Gori argues that they were sacred offerings, *donaria*, suspended in honour of Jove, but produces little evidence in support of this theory, while Passer agrees with Heydemann that the ladder certainly represented the goddess Fortuna.

We repeat that in every case in which the ladder is depicted on these Apulian vases it appears in close connection with a love scene, denoted always by a winged Eros. Moreover, so far as the present writer is aware, it is not found as an ancient symbol, or indeed at all in classic pictures, except upon the *dischi sacri* of Taranto in Apulia, and upon Apulian Greek vases. Yet it is found to-day as a modern Neapolitan *porta fortuna*, or, as we call it, a charm.

We therefore with some confidence maintain that it represents upon the vases the ladder of Fortune (Heydemann says, in successful love), and that upon the *dischi sacri*, pronounced by experts to be contemporary with the vases in the same district, the ladder is to be taken as having the same meaning.

It should here be remembered in this connection, that we have already remarked upon the apparently licentious character of many of the pantheistic hands, and knowing what we do of Roman society of about the date of those hands—say the time of the prosperity of Pompeii—we are not doing the earlier people of Apulia, who used the *dischi sacri*, an injustice if we attribute much the same character to the symbols on the latter.

Fig. 144 is another small but very interesting perfect disc. Here again we have a very few, but very large, separate symbols. It will be noted that Jove's unmistakable thunderbolt has appeared so far on every one of the foregoing examples, and it will be remembered on how many of the hands it appeared upon the tips of the fingers. Once again in this persistence of the thunderbolt we find a striking connection between the *dischi sacri* and the *mani pantée*. The ladder here holds a very subordinate position; still, it is present. The distaff, single and large, is an important feature, not only on this plaque but on Fig. 139, and on several others in our collection. On these, as well as on this last (Fig. 144), it is placed next to the club of Hercules, and therefore we must assume its position to be intentional

Fig. 144. Terra-cotta Disc found at Taranto (1/2 linear).

and important, as it is undoubtedly on Figs. 131, 136. Of course the distaff has always been commonly looked on as representing Clotho (the spinner), one of the Fates, but on several of these discs we find three small distaffs together, and it is of course but reasonable to assume that the three Parcae were thereby designated. But upon the same plaques (*e.g.*, Figs. 133, 134, 135, 139), and on several others in the author's collection, we find this large single distaff, as well as the three small ones, and we submit that it must represent some special one of the greater deities. This can only be Athene (Minerva), the patroness of spinning and weaving. Besides the distaff, she also among the greater gods was represented by the Cock.

It is of much interest to compare the reverence implied upon these discs, by the difference in importance accorded to the several symbols. Thus, on Figs. 141, 144, two unbroken examples with few upon each, we note four, common to both, *e.g.*, ladder, club, thunderbolt, *caduceus*, and the two uncertain figures; but while on Fig. 141 these are all about equal in prominence, on Fig. 144 the thunderbolt and *caduceus* largely predominate, whereas the ladder and two doubtful figures are much reduced, and the distaff on the latter is substituted for the open hand. The hand above the thunderbolt on 141 we interpret as the sign of triumph and victory, upon which we have before remarked. The two undetermined objects on Figs. 141, 145 are probably the same as the one on Fig. 144, but their extreme prominence on Fig. 141 forbids us to adopt the method of Jahn and others—to pass them by unnoticed. This figure is given in Montfaucon as one of the signs of Venus, an alternative of the well-known *ankh*, still used as her astronomical sign. It is then suggested that Aphrodite may be the goddess typified on these discs by this doubtful symbol—we have before suggested the resemblance to the sign of the "ascending node," but we shall be glad of a better interpretation.

Of the object looking like the number 8 on several plaques we cannot even suggest an explanation. Both the figures above referred to will be found upon the hands.

The last of our illustrations (Fig. 145) is of the wheel or radiated type, of comparatively large dimensions (7¾ in. diameter), and in extremely low relief, so that as a mould it would be absurdly useless for making any sort of raised figures upon sacrificial cakes, or

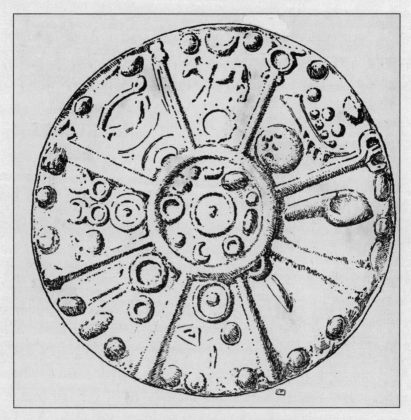

Fig. 145. Terra-cotta Disc found at Taranto (1/2 linear).

HORNS OF HONOR

upon any soft substance. Although a complete disc, the figures are too indistinct to be more than very partially identified. We note the scabbard, trident, and *caduceus*, with the club and perhaps the torch, but three of the radii cannot be guessed at. There seem to be several crescents; a sheep is distinct, and so are the two signs of Venus or the ascending node(?). There is a triangle and a squat two-handled vase, both of which are found upon the hands (Figs. 97, 114); but this example lends us very little help towards determining the purpose or intention of these strange objects, for we must maintain that so many ancient designs, all of the same general character and having so many traits in common, must have had a distinct use, and must have entered into the daily life of the people.

The diversity of size we find in them, seems at first sight to point to a variety of uses, and if the many fragments we have were indeed patterns, it may well be that the finished casts, in whatever material they were made, were applied to various purposes. The shape of Figs. 133, 134, 141, with many other similar ones taken in connection with their smaller sizes, seems strongly to point to their having been patterns of moulds for making the upper side of the common lamp of the period; but of these lamps none have been found at Taranto, though many have turned up elsewhere.

We cannot, however, identify any known lamp as made from any one of these moulds. Even if we could do so, we are met with the difficulty: What about the finished reliefs, Figs. 133 and 134, and the others we know of? In support of the lamp theory—for we have many casts from actual moulds, very nearly like Figs. 133 and 134— we produce a drawing (Fig. 146) of a lamp having upon it many of the symbols found on the discs. Another lamp is depicted in the

Fig. 146. Terra-cotta Lamp.

same work with very similar objects upon it. This lamp (Fig. 146) is of later date than the *dischi sacri*, and is probably contemporary with the hands. We find upon it, however, many of the symbols found alike upon both discs and hands. At the top we have the face of the sun, apparently mounted on a swivel, of which the supporter is the crescent. The central seated figure is unquestionably Fortuna, who holds her cornucopia in the left hand, while holding out a *patera* in the right.

Very many of these patera are shown on the discs, but we do not see any plausible explanation for them when appearing as in this case alone. Upon this lamp we find two serpents, a peacock (Juno), a dolphin (Neptune), an eagle, a dove (Aphrodite), thyrsus, *caduceus*, pomegranates (Hera and Demeter),[94] cymbals, ear of corn (Ceres), pincers, *systrum*, lyre, club, torch—indeed, as many symbols as on the discs, and of course representing as large a pantheon. The border too has a very Greek feeling, although the lamp is distinctly Roman.

Another use, for which we suggest these moulds may have been used, is that from them bronze mirrors may have been cast. In Montfaucon are plates of many mirror backs of Roman period with symbols upon them of like character, though none precisely like any found on these discs. Seyffert too gives a drawing of a mirror of similar character. Moreover, the backs of modern Japanese mirrors of today bear many objects, such as a tortoise, fish, cross of leaves, birds, placed in no apparent connection or design, just as we find the same objects as symbols upon the hands and discs. In one or two cases the objects are identical. Backs of mirrors then is another use put forward to account for some of the moulds. Many of the plaques are far too large for either of these purposes, which could only have been adopted for the smaller sizes. These large ones are fragments of circles, and not of the pear-shape suitable for lamps or mirrors. It is suggested that these were moulds for embossed dishes, of which there are still large numbers of fragments to be seen at Naples and elsewhere. These dishes are of red pottery, such as might be cast from the kind of moulds we possess. They have serpents, frogs, lizards, swords, and various like objects embossed upon them, and we suggest they may be the prototypes from whence Palissy got his ideas, if not his technique. The large dishes of Greco-Roman Taranto, of which we have the moulds, were of course many centuries earlier in date than the fragments to be seen at Naples (also a part of Magna Graecia), but the general similarity is quite unmistakable.

What, however, we repeat, is to be said of the small finished plaques in relief, such as our Figs. 130 and 131? Again we have to look at modern facts to explain ancient analogies. We have already shown that an artificial horn of terra-cotta was made for suspension in ancient Tarentum. To-day in the grocers' and butchers' shops of modern Taranto and Naples may be seen a terra-cotta horn attached to a crescent, a ball and a hand, hung up over the door or under the ceiling, avowedly to keep off the evil eye. The writer possesses several; they are painted bright red. Moreover, Canon Jorio expressly refers to these amulets suspended by Neapolitan shopkeepers, and we have before alluded to many of these same symbols made in Caldas ware, in Portugal, intended to be placed against a wall. We have then in the shops, on the Cimaruta for the children's necks, or as separate charms, sold openly *contro malocchio*, most of the very same symbols found upon the discs, and later upon the *mano pantea*. Is it then presumptuous to maintain that one important use for these terra-cotta plaques was to attach them to the interior walls of houses as sacred appeals to the protecting deities represented, against the ever-dreaded evil eye?[95] We believe this to have been the prime object of the terra-cottas, and that subsequently the same devices were used for the same purpose by way of decoration on lamps, mirrors, and dishes. The like or similar symbols were embossed later on the bronze hands, and exist to-day as charms, not only in half-heathen Naples, but in Christian England, and more or less in most other countries. We are fortified in our contention (written long before we had read his remarks) by Heydemann, who agrees with none of the modern writers who have referred to these objects, and maintains that their sole use and object was apotropaic; that is protective as averters of evil. He considers they were suspended in the houses where found to keep off ill influences, and this he says is proved by the crowd of divinities represented.

Lastly we venture to submit that we have proved our only assumption—the one with which we started on page 1, that all ornament or decoration had originally some distinct signification; and that we have produced pictorial as well as literary facts, which throw light upon the life and manners of the obscure past.

ENDNOTES

CHAPTER 1

1   The immense importance it has acquired as an expressive prefix, and the endless uses in which the word *head* enters into our everyday speech, can best be understood by a study of the many pages devoted to it in the new *Historical English Dictionary.*

2   The question as to whether the domestic cock existed in Europe in very early times is beyond the range of our subject. The fact, however, that a store of legend and tradition had grown up around it in Pliny's time, proves it to have been familiar in ages quite remote enough for our purpose.

3   Excellent examples of this exaggerated crest, though without the horns, will be found in O. Jahn's *Uber Darst. Griech. Dicht. auf Vasen-bildern*; in *Ab. d. Kön. Sächs. Ges. d. Wis.*, 8r B., Leipzig, 1861; also in Sittl's *Gebärden d. Gr. u. Röm.*, Leipzig, 1890, p. 321.

4   If this statement be challenged, we will leave experts to decide the question as to whether animals and the forces of nature upon earth were not the first to be worshipped. Probably they were, for primitive man was always more inclined to propitiate the powers he knew best, and most dreaded, by his worship or sacrifice, than to show gratitude to those from whence he believed his good things to come.

5   Compare especially all Murillo's pictures of the Assumption at Madrid, of which the Louvre example is a fair type.

6   On p. 541 is Bel Merodach, with a thunderbolt in each hand, fighting with a griffin, *i.e.*, the power of evil. Professor Driver, in *Authority and Archaeology*, writes this god as Marduk (p. 122 *et al.*).

7   In all the Scandinavian tongues, like the Teutonic, the moon is masculine and the sun feminine.

8   King, *Gnostics*, p. 65. *Cf.* also account of the introduction of the worship of Serapis and Isis from Alexandria, *Evil Eye*, p. 302.

9   "Tauri primogeniti."

10 Vulgate, "Rhinocerotis."

11 The frontispiece to the writer's copy of Delrio's *De Magia*, 1603, shows Moses with conspicuous horns, when with Aaron he is standing before the Almighty, and also in eight other of the scenes representing the plagues of Egypt; in every case before the Exodus, and long before his descent from the Mount. Torreblanca's *De Magia* has a frontispiece showing the same scenes though differently treated. In each, Moses has horns distinctly portrayed. These curious anachronisms do but support the evidence of the belief in actual concrete horns.

12 "Hi, ut firmius consisteret, illum sub mento duabus hinc et inde vittis constringebant. Sulpitio, inquit Valerius Maximus, Sacerdotium abrogatum fuit, quia sacrificanti apex de capite deciderat." Montfaucon, ii. p. 39.

13 It has been objected that there is no evidence of the Macedonians wearing horned helmets. The famous portrait of Alexander at the battle of Issus in the great mosaic at Naples shows him without helmet; but inasmuch as we have plenty of horned Greek helmets in the concrete bronze of about the date of the Macedonian, and have besides the legend above cited, we must leave the question to be settled by experts.

14 For this suggestion I am indebted to Mr. J. L. Myres, in an address at the British Association (Section H) at Liverpool, 1897.

15 Clazomenæ means "the screaming swans."— Fraser, *Pausanias*, iv. p. 121.

16 See H.E. D.t s.v. "Chaplet."

17 See Smith's *Dict.*, *cit. s.v.*, "Phaleræ," for further information on this subject.

18 Examples of all are given in Montfaucon, iv. p. 103, and in Seyffert's *Dictionary of Antiquities*.

19 This cannot be true, though all are apparently by the same hand, probably painted in the fifteenth century, for the reason that some are portraits of men who lived long after Tommaso degli Stefani. But for our purpose, the later the painting the better for our contention.

20 Grose, in *Dictionary of Buckish Slang*, 1811, has "Actæon, a cuckold; from the horns placed upon the head of Actaeon by Diana." In a seventeenth century book (*Paradoxical Assertions and Philosophical Problems*, by R.H., 1659) is a chapter headed "Why are cuckolds said to wear horns?" The author says, "Is it not because the abused cuckold becomes lunatick at the affront, and so every moon at least, being either changeable, jealous, or horn mad, or all

three, he wears horns by assimulation?" Captain Bourke says (*Scatologic Rites of all Nations*, p. 408), "The horns of honor of the deities worshipped by women who were ordered by their husbands to become religious prostitutes were transferred to the husband: what had been the outward sign of extreme devotion and self-abnegation was turned into ridicule and opprobrium."

21 *Corriere da Napoli*, September 18th, 1896.

22 *Order of Consecration of a Bishop Elect* (*imprimatur* H. Card. Vaughan), p. 14. Burns and Oates, 1893. Copies of this can be obtained in the original Latin as well as in the translation as above.

CHAPTER II

23 "For ye provoked him that made you by sacrificing unto devils, and not to God." (Baruch iv. 7.) Satan is also mentioned in Sirach (Ecclesiasticus) xxi. 27.

24 This is no romance. One of the demons depicted in the picture by Jan Brueghel, referred to later (p. 182), has in the foreground a tortoise with a man's face and feet, besides many other monstrosities.

25 Now in the British Museum.

26 Such a representation is to be seen in *Le Kalendier des Bergers*, Lyon, 1504 (Claude Nourry). This figure is altogether hideous; both hands and feet are claws, while the head is absolutely nondescript. The body, arms, and legs are human, but above all are the horns of a goat. Pictures of this kind must be quite familiar to our readers, and we need, therefore, only allude to them.

27 *Disquisitionum Magicarum*, lib. ii. p. 141: "Solent Malefici et Lamiæ cum demonibus, illi quidem succubis; hae vero incubis; actum Venerium exercere." Delrio sums up his argument with "Dirimus ergo. Ex concubitu incubi cum muliere aliquando prolem nasci posse; et tum prolis verum patrem non fore daemonem, sed ilium hominem cujus femine daemon abusus merit."

28 E. A. de Cosson, *The Cradle of the Blue Nile*, 1877, vol. ii. p. 73.

29 Early English Text Society.

30 A story of the devil and his bride, very different to this, told by an old negro in New Orleans, is published in the *Journal of American Folklore*, No. xlv. 1899, p. 128.

31 Those who desire to study this curious phase in religious history will find much information in Buckle's chapter on "An Examination of Scotch Intellect in the Seventeenth Century," *Civilisation*, vol iii. p. 191 *et seq*.

32 "The devil damn thee black, thou cream fac'd loon."—*Macbeth*, v. iii.

33 See Bochart, *Hierosoicon*, Leipzig, 1794, especially *De Lepore* (Lev. xi. 6, Deut. xiv. 7), vol. ii. p. 400. The devil especially assumed the shape of the unclean animals.

34 Letter from Miss Underhill to the writer, published in Devon Association's *Report on Folk-lore*, 1896, p. 95.

35 *Laus Asini*, Leyden, quoted by Gubernatis.

36 Seneca, *Oedipus*. See also *Handbuch der Deutschen Mythologie*.

37 We cannot account for the vermilion colour, unless it represents a new conception based on Faust, being usually clothed in red. It should, however, be noted that cows', rams', and terra-cotta horns and hands hung up in Naples shops, of which the writer has several specimens, are painted bright red, so are the hands over Jewish doors in Jerusalem. Red and blue seem to be prophylactic colours; *cf.* red coral.

38 Matthew xvi. 24.

39 See an article in *Mélusine*, September, 1896, p. 100, "Le Serpent d'Airan et le livre des secrets d'Enoch"; also *The Book of Enoch*, translated by Morfill and Charles, Oxford, 1896.

40 On the Griffin, "The watcher of the gold," see Pliny, *Nat. Hist.* vii. 2, xxxiii. 42; Milton, *Par. Lost*, ii. l. 943; also Schliemann, *Mycenae*, pp. 177–8. "Griffins are beasts like lions, but with the wings and beak of an eagle." They are on the helmet of Athena of the Parthenon. "Aristias of Proconnesus says in his poem that these griffins fight for the gold with the (one-eyed) Arimaspians . . . and that the gold which the griffins guard is produced from the earth."—Frazer, *Pausanias*, vol. i. book i. p. 35.

41 It is quite possible that the Scala griffins may be ancient Roman from some temple. Columns and pieces of sculpture from earlier work are often found in later buildings.

42 On the Babylonish belief in the creation and fall of man, see Smith, *Chaldean Account of Genesis*, p. 87 *et seq.*

43 This wood-cut is not in the print room at the British Museum nor mentioned in any notice of Dürer's works.

44 King, *Gnostics*, p. 83; *Symbolica Dianae Ephesia*, p. 10: "Apuleius quoque Isin, Deûm Matrem, Minervam, Junonem, Hecatem, Cerem, Venerem, Proserpinam, Hecatem unam, eandemque esse praedicat."

45 On this subject see Martin, *Histoire des Monstres*, pp. 309 *et seq.*; also King,

Gnostics, See also Is. Geoffroy Saint-Hilaire, *Dictionnaire des Sciences médi-cales, s.v.* "Hermaphrodisme." It seems to be the verdict of science that though physiologically possible and in many animals even *tres accentué,* it is quite unknown amongst birds, but whether occurring in animals or man it is always teratologous.

The present writer, however, has seen pheasants whose plumage very distinctly partook of both sexes, and he is informed by gamekeepers and others that such hermaphrodite birds are not uncommon.

46 Upon the word mask the writer was severely criticised for stating in the *Evil Eye,* p. 147, that "it is said to be but a corruption of the older Greek βασκα, whence βασκανα, *fascina* or amulets."

He was told that he was utterly wrong—that the word is Arabic, etc.

With all deference to modern dictionaries, he begs to repeat what he said as above, and to say that his book not being a philological treatise he did not think it necessary to give his authority, but for the information of those who believe the word to be Arabic he refers them to Boettiger, *Kleine Schriften,* Dresden, 1838, Ueber das Wort "Maske," vol. iii. p. 402; also *ib.* ii. p. 366.

See also Boettiger, *Opuscula,* Dresden, 1837, p. 222 n., "De Personis Scenicis: vulgo Larvis."

Lobeck, *Aglaophamus,* p. 973 n., says of "Graeci novitii μασκαρεμαγα appellant, *i.e.,* larvas":

"Nomen romanicum Maaca s. Mascara s. Talamasca cum latino fascinum (unde fescenninum derivant) et graeco βασκειν κακολογειν βασκαινειν, βασκα, cognatum esse veterum Etymologorum conjectura est haud improbabilis; quanquam Reiskius in Act.—Jenens, t iv. p. 160, arabicum putat." Boettiger, however, writes decidedly, and ridicules the Arabic theory.

47 See *West Somerset Word Book, s.v.* "Soce."

CHAPTER III

48 Jorio, *Mimichi degli Antichi.*

49 A great deal on this subject is said by Marion Crawford, in his novel Pietro Ghisleri, vol. ii. p. 30 *et seq.*

50 Psalm cxxxiv. 2, cxli. 2, and many other passages. The "lifting up," in these passages, refers to the Jewish method dealt with later.

51 This gesture is described by Canon Jorio, see *Evil Eye,* pp. 274–5, as having a three-fold significance—justice, perfection, threatening, when held

horizontally, and of love when uplifted. It cannot then be far-fetched to conclude that the special rubric ordering this position takes note of the mystical though pagan significance of the gesture, and thereby symbolises the Holy Trinity in the act of benediction during mass.

52 Exodus xxix. 20, Leviticus viii. 33, 24. See also Prætorius, *De Pollice*, Leipzig, 1677, p. 101. Much information can be obtained from this book.

53 Compare this with the Moslem pilgrim described post, p. 173.

54 Figs. 64, 65 are from Twining's, *Symbols and Emblems of Early and Mediæval Christian Art*, Pl. II., 16, 19, where a large number of these gestures may be studied. It is possible, though not so stated, that Fig. 64 may be from a Greek, and not a Latin, MS.

55 See Wilkinson, *Ancient Egyptians*, iii. 425, "An attitude of devotion," Thebes. Two figures are shown lifting up both hands. Abundant examples of this and other attitudes may be found in the many illustrations of Egyptian paintings and sculpture.

56 *Times* Report of Inauguration of Mr. McKinley, March 5, 1897.

57 In the Vulgate we read a triumphal arch, "fornicem triumphalem," and in the R.V. "a monument," but both the Hebrew and Septuagint say distinctly "hand." This is given in the margin of the R.V.

58 A. J. Evans, Address to Section H. at British Association, Liverpool, 1897.

59 From Montfaucon, vol. iii. Suppl., pl. 44. See also pl. 70. Several of the weights have a similar hand upon them with a roundel for each ounce. Priapus was dearly a patron divinity of Roman traders. Many of the weights bear phallic symbols on the obverse, with an open hand and club or hook on the reverse. A lyre, a dolphin, a thunderbolt, and other well-known symbols occur along with the open hand on weights of the time of the empire.

60 The writer is indebted for the above to his friend Sir James Campbell, of Rosneath, whose long residence in the East renders his information of much value.

61 "Signa que dat digites medio cum pollice junctes," Fasti, v. 433; "Favebant ii, qui manum in obscaenum modum formabunt," Prætorius, *De Pollice*, Leipzig, 1677, p. 42.

62 Among Neapolitans the position of the hands has all-important meanings, and those who desire full information on the subject are referred to Canon Jorio's *Mimica degli Antichi*, from which are reproduced three interesting plates of gestures, with their several significations, in *The Evil Eye*, p. 274 *et seq*.

63 Letter from J. B. Andrews, February 5, 1895.

64 Grose, *Prov. Gloss. and Popular Superstitions*; Brand, *Pop. Antiq.* iii. 278; Henderson, *Folk-lore of Northern Europe*, p. 202; Baring-Gould, *Curious Myths of the Middle Ages*, p. 405. All these copy from Collin de Plancy, *Dictionnaire Infernal*, who first obtained it from *Les Secrets du Petit Albert*. On comparing these translations with the original, we find all exactly alike, and none exact. We therefore subjoin the original from *Les Secrets du Petit Albert*, Lion, 1754, p. 111:—

"On prend la main droite ou la gauche d'un pendu exposé sur les grands chemins; on l'enveloppe dans un morceau de drap mortuaire, dans lequel on la presse bien pour lui faire rendre le peu de sang qui pouvoit etre resté, puis on la met dans une vase de terre avec du limat, du salpêtre, du sel, et du poivre long, le tout bien pulverisé; on la laisse durant quinze jours dans ce pot, puis l'ayant tirée on l'expose au grand Soleil de la Canicule, jusqu'a ce qu'elle soit bien sèche, et si la soleil ne suffit pas, on la met dans un four qui soit chauffé avec la Fougere et la Vervaine, puis on compose une espèce de chandelle avec de la graisse de pendu, de la cire vierge, et du sisamie de Laponie, et l'on sert de cette main de gloire comme d'un chandelier, pour y tenir cette chandelle allumée, et dans tous les lieux ou l'on va avec ce funeste instrument, ceux qui y font demeurer immobiles. Et sur ce qu'on leur demanda s'il n'y avoit point de remèdé pour se guarantir de ce prestige, ils dirent que la Main de gloire devenoit sans effet, et que les Voleurs ne pourrvient s'en servir si l'on frottoit le seuil de la porte de la maison, ou les autres endroits par ou ils peuvent entrer avec un onguent composé, de sul de Chat noir, de graisse de Poule blanche, et du sang de Chouetse, et qu'il falloit que cette confection fût faite dans le temps de la Canicule."

65 The witches' Sabbath was supposed to be held on a Saturday, when there was a general assembly to worship their master the devil, who appeared in the form of a goat, by dancing around him. At some of these assemblies it is said that Satan was much out of humour, and that he vented his spleen by beating the witches black and blue with the spits and brooms on which they had ridden to the tryst. Before the meeting breaks up all are said to have had the honour of saluting the devil's posterior. They afterwards open graves to obtain ingredients for their incantations from the dead bodies; also at the Sabbath "Satan teacheth how to make pictures of wax or clay, that by roasting thereof, the persons that they bear the name of may be continually melted or dried away by continual sickness." (King James, *Dæmonology*, bk. ii. chap, v.) See also Scott, *Discovery*

of Witchcraft, bk. iii. chap. i. p. 40 (Ed. B. Nicholson. Pub. by E. Stock, London, 1886, pp. 34–37.) Collin de Plancy (*Dict. Infernal*, p. 252 *et seq.*; a long account will be found here) says that on the spot where witches have held their Sabbath, nothing will grow, and that Strozzi declares that he saw on a field near Vicenza a circle surrounding a chestnut tree, as barren as the sands of Libya, where witches had danced and held their Sabbaths. Wednesday and Thursday are the ordinary nights for the meeting. All of both sexes have a mark impressed by the devil *entre les fesses*. Part of the ceremony is *baiser le posterieur de Maitre Leonard*. A witch being asked if she had kissed him said he had a *visage entre le cul et la queue*, and that it was this they kissed, not the *cul*. [**Elworthy presents the common misguided vilification of Witches in this passage, much of which has no foundation in anything factual. However, it seems apparent that someone disguised in horned animal costume was involved in the old rites of Witchcraft. Dancing was certainly a part of such rites, and according to oral legend some Witches used the title "devil" for the horned figure (mostly likely in defiance toward Christianity and its dictates). In a curious old rural practice, trees were beaten with sticks in the belief that it stimulated the production of fruit/nuts. Perhaps the misunderstanding of such practices led some commentators on Witchcraft to believe that Witches were beating each other with broomsticks in the woods where they gathered. In a likewise manner, old ritual fertility practices may also have lent to misunderstandings among the outsiders.**]

66 For the loan of the two engravings, under discussion here, the writer is indebted to his friend the Rev. S. Baring-Gould.

67 Southey, *Thalaba the Destroyer*, book v. 37. In a note to the writer's copy (Longmans' ed., 1853) is given a long extract from Grose, *Prov. Gloss.*, with the often copied translation from Collin de Plancy, mistakes and all.

68 *Gentleman's Magazine*, April, 1887, "A Strange Crime," by Rev. S. Baking-Gould, to whom the present writer is indebted for several hints on this subject.

69 From letter signed C. B. Loughborough, January 18 (1889?) in *Telegraph*.

70 Shakespeare evidently knew of this belief:—

"We steal as in a castle, cock-sure; we have the receipt of fern-seed, we
   walk invisible.

"Chamberlain.—Nay, by my faith, I think you are more beholden to
   the night than to fern-seed for your walking invisible."

—Henry IV. ii. 1.

71 Leader in morning paper (? *Telegraph*), Jan. 14, 15, 1889.

Chapter IV

72 See Bonomi, *Nineveh and its Palaces*, p. 253.

73 *Mittheilungen der Antiq. Gesellschaft*, band xi. 7, pp. 35, 37. Zurich. We give Meyer's quotation, for we are unable to find it in the *Metamorphoses* of Apuleius.

74 Acts xiv. 12.

75 Réville, *The Devil, his Origin and Greatness*, trs. 1877, p. 3.

76 Sittl, *op. cit.*, refers to these hands, and follows all the rest in calling them Votivhanden. He refers (p. 325) to Jahn, Meyer, Becker, and others; especially he refers to three bronze hands discussed by Karl Dilthey, *Arch. epigr. Mitth. aus Oesterreich*, ii. 1877.

77 Montfaucon, ii. p. 249.

78 Montfaucon, Appendix, vol. iv. p. 119.

79 *Pretorius De Pollice*, p. 211. Osiris usually holds a whip, in Egyptian sculptures.

80 "Sacri tripodes viridesque coronae."—Virgil, *Aen.*, v. 110.

81 This is being done to a large extent in Southern Italy, petroleum has so completely superseded olive-oil for lamps.

82 Compare the famous column made of twisted serpents from Delphi, now on the Atmeidan at Constantinople. See *Evil Eye*, p. 314.

83 Frogs and toads were both considered powerful aphrodisiacs, and entered largely into the components of love philtres; they seem, like lizard and crocodile, to have been treated as identical when used symbolically. Potter, *Ant. Graec.*, ii. 248, speaks of the virtues in the bones of the right and left sides of a toad, very much to the same effect as Pliny, *Nat. Hist.*, 32 (vol. vi. p. 22, Bohn), does of the frog. He evidently got his idea from Pliny, and translated toad, whereas Bohn's translator calls it frog.

84 Iamblicus, *Vita Pythag.*, cap. xxvii. Heliodorus, *Aethiop.*, cap. iii.; also Iamblicus, *On the Mysteries*, etc, translated by Taylor, 1895, p. 240. Much information is to be found in this book upon several of the symbols of the gods; especially in a translation of *Dissertation on Theurgy*, by Proclus, p. 343 *et seq.* In this we learn also the symbolic meaning of certain flowers, such as heliotropes, the lotus, etc. We are also told how the cock is much feared by the lion—that there are many demons with a leonine front, who, when a cock is placed before them (p. 345), suddenly disappear.

85 Liceto, *De Lucernis Antiquorum*, p. 1179 (1652).

86 Liceto, *De Lucernis Antiquorum*, p. 1179 (1652).

87 It is assumed from these, by Jahn, that all the hands on which they appear are *ex votos* in respect of childbirth, past or expectant. Against this we have Meyer's remarks (*ante*, p. 245), which seem to be conclusive.

88 In the Naples Museum are several statues of Isis, each holding a *sistrum*.

89 Knowing what we do of Roman society at the period, whenever there is any doubt of the intention of a symbol, it is safe to ascribe it to the more licentious divinity.

90 For the sketch from the original, whence this illustration is drawn, the author is indebted to his friend Mr. Strangman. All others are from the author's own drawings from the original hands, unless where otherwise described.

91 The worship of Castor and Pollux was held in high esteem in Rome, at and before the time of these hands.

92 Genesis xxxi. 19.

CHAPTER V

93 *Lexikon der griech. und röm. Mythologie*, "Bestehend aus zwei vertikalen, durch zwei horizontalen verbundenen Balken."

94 Frazer, *Pausanias*, ii. 7, 4 (vol. i. p. 96). The pomegranate in the hand of Hera. *Ibid.*, viii. 37, 4 (vol. iv. p. 380). Those initiated into the Eleusinian Mysteries were forbidden to eat the pomegranate; perhaps it was a symbol of Persephone rather than Demeter. Demeter was symbolised by a fig-tree, which she presented to Phytalus. On this see Frazer, *ibid.*, i. 37, 2.

95 See *ante*, p. 59. Advertisement from *Italian Journal* of 1896.

ABOUT THE AUTHOR

FREDERICK THOMAS ELWORTHY was a noted scholar, folklorist, and antiquarian. His other books include *The Evil Eye* (1895).

ABOUT THE EDITOR

RAVEN GRIMASSI is a neo-pagan scholar and the author of 17 books about witchcraft and the occult. He is an avid researcher on folklore and folk magic practices, particularly in European cultures. He is currently the co-director of Elder of the Ash, Birch and Willow System of Old World Witchery. Visit him at *www.ravengrimassi.net*.

TO OUR READERS

Weiser Books, an imprint of Red Wheel/Weiser, publishes books across the entire spectrum of occult, esoteric, speculative, and New Age subjects. Our mission is to publish quality books that will make a difference in people's lives without advocating any one particular path or field of study. We value the integrity, originality, and depth of knowledge of our authors.

Our readers are our most important resource, and we appreciate your input, suggestions, and ideas about what you would like to see published.

Visit our website at *www.redwheelweiser.com* to learn about our upcoming books and free downloads, and be sure to go to *www.redwheelweiser.com/newsletter* to sign up for newsletters and exclusive offers.

You can also contact us at *info@rwwbooks.com* or at

Red Wheel/Weiser, LLC
665 Third Street, Suite 400
San Francisco, CA 94107